Life Remixed

Understanding The Journey of Success

Your college degree does not make you successful.

Your job does not make you successful.

Owning a home does not make you successful.

Success is determined by your ability to make a profound and lasting change in the lives of others.

Saideh Browne

For we do not wrestle against flesh and blood;
but against the rulers,
against the authorities,
against the cosmic powers
over this present darkness,
[but] against the spiritual forces of evil
in the heavenly places.
Ephesians 6:12

Life Remixed
Understanding the Journey of Success
Copyright © 2012 by Saideh Browne
First Printing April 2012

ISBN: 978-0979364266

Published by
GS Publishing Group

This book is available at special discounts for churches, schools, and other educational institutions.
Contact GS Publishing Group
201-263-4300

Author Bookings and Management
saidehbrowne@gmail.com

This book is dedicated to Barshea
Reach for the stars!

A special *thank you* to my fitness team
who readied my body for the book tour
Teresa J.D.
Rocky
Alton
Daryl
Nilsa
Janae

An extra special *thank you* to my Life Remixed Radio,
now Sai Browne Morning Show, family
DeJuan Boyd for rockin' it out with me since day one

Djuan Coleon for all of your advice and spiritual insight

Dee Dee Cocheta for your PR support
for the show and all of my projects

Celeste a.k.a. CQ a.k.a Curvy Queen
for your social media support and friendship ☺

Saideh Browne's Other Books

99 Tips to Transform Your Business Today

How To Make Motivational Speaking Your Day Job

100 Words of Wisdom for Women (contributor)

From Hip-Hop to Heaven for Girls

From Hip-Hop to Heaven

Can Hip-Hop be Holy?

Live DVD Recording
From Hip-Hop to Heaven
Youth Empowerment
Conference

Table of Contents

Throughout the book you will see the following symbols; here is their meaning.

⧗ Something for you to think about

▤ Something you should take note of

✍ A place for you to take notes in the book

👍 A special tip from me to you

Prologue

I wrote *Life Remixed* to document and better understand my spiritual journey and better understand the correlation between my faith and the good and bad things that are happening in the world today. I was born during a time when changing jobs like one changes underwear was considered haram (a Muslim term for something really, really bad); but now, a cross section of jobs, skills and acquired knowledge may deem you more valuable to the ever elusive interview with a hiring manager.

Life Remixed started out as scribbled notes on little pieces of paper. I'd write every time God sent me a message that I felt could help me better navigate my life. Over time, I realized I was not the only person trying to sort out this new, global, not private world in which we now find ourselves existing in. This book is truly four years in the making. I dipped and dodged my responsibility and obligation to share with you my findings. I thought I was crazy and wanted to figure this out on my own so people would continue to think I really had it all together. See, writing this book would be an indictment on the perception I perpetuate that I really have my shit together (don't worry, there's only a few curses in the book).

I have been lied to since birth, we all have. I realized it a long time ago but never felt my discovery important enough to share how I knew, why I knew and if what I knew even mattered; at least to anyone else but me anyway.

Life Remixed is about all of us learning to navigate in the new world in which we live. Those in power have had this planned for some time and we were all just pawns in their game. I could have been one of them; in fact, my family wanted me to be one of them but I chose to vibe with the people. Maybe one day I will be given a mic large enough to influence the masses; but until that day comes I will continue to share what I know via books, media appearances and speaking engagements. God knows what's in store for me. I want us to all be happy but at this moment in time, happiness is seemingly elusive. But, really, it's not. Happiness is all around us, in all things and most importantly is grounded in truth. The more we are truthful to ourselves and others the happier we are over time.

God wants us to happy and have a peace-filled life but we self-sabotage and then get angry because we didn't seek the truth in all things and all situations. I am a messenger and a bringer of truth and light. I know God will reveal the answer to every single question you have but you must have some skin in the game and start the journey. I have so much to share, so much to tell and so much invisible energy to receive from you as you read this book. May God bless you, me and all of the people whose lives we collectively touch. This is my 7th book, thank you for reading it.

Blessings

Section
One

What Happened?

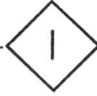

What Happened?

Don't go around saying the world owes you a living.
The world owes you nothing. It was here first.
Mark Twain

I remember thinking one afternoon, "What ever happened to JaRule?" Ah, then I remembered, 50 Cent happened to JaRule! The Rule reigned supreme over Hip-Hop culture and the music charts for some years, and then 50 arrived on the scene. After a few publicized words between the two New York rappers and the rise of 50's Q rating, sadly, JaRule was no more.

The same can be said for the America we've known since we were kids. The American Dream could be ours if we worked hard, waited our turn and always did the right thing. Then September 2008 crashed in, literally, and destroyed many lives just like 50 did to Ja; and for no apparent reason. I'd love to blame what has happened in our country on globalization, the technological divide and with most emphasis American International Group, Bank of America, Merrill Lynch, Fannie Mae, Freddie Mac, Lehman Brothers, the fall of the Dow Jones Industrial Average by over 500 points in one day, The Federal Reserve's billion-dollar loans, but sadly, I cannot. I blame people, us included.

During the mortgage crisis, a cable TV talking head said that people should have read their mortgage applications more carefully and probably knew what they were signing and signed anyway. In theory that sounds pretty accurate, but in practice it's ludicrous. Because of the food we consume, the manner in which computers have sped up our daily lives and other factors, no one wants to sit for forty-five minutes to read jargon they may or may not understand anyway. True wealth belongs to those who are patient.

Can you solve this math question? Two trains leave the station at the same time, one heading west and the other east. The Westbound train travels 20 miles per hour slower than the eastbound train. If the two trains are 900 miles apart after five hours, what is the rate of the westbound train?

The eastbound train (A) speed = x mph
The westbound train (B) speed will be x-20 mph

Distance = speed * time
Distance traveled by train A = 5x
Distance traveled by train B = 5*(x-20)

5x+5(x-20) = 900
5x+5x-100 = 900
10x=900+100
10x=1000
 x=100 mph eastbound train
westbound train = 100-20=80 mph

The calculations detailed show how to solve a basic algebraic equation. Whether you arrived at the correct answer or not is not my point, but whether you knew *how* to position the facts and think through the process to ultimately arrive at the correct answer. The key to solving algebraic equations is properly placing the given facts. Once the facts are properly placed the answer is within the problem-solvers grasp; but one misplaced belief of where the numbers should go will throw off the entire solution solving experience and the correct answer will forever remain elusive and a mystery.

There is no time left to be depressed, bitter and angry; today is the day you give yourself permission to slow down and properly place the facts given to you. Those who are capable enough to solve the most basic problems challenging their existence remain mindful that they probably don't have all of the facts or enough accurate information to successfully deconstruct the complexities of the problems that lay ahead of all of us. Don't fret, it's not just you; it's designed this way.

I took a cooking class, learned how to sew and balance a checkbook all in the 7th grade - we used to be taught *to* think. Now, we're fed *what* to think, and in doing so, have allowed others (or computers) to do the thinking for us. As we become more aware of the travesties of justice happening all around us many of us don't even know where to begin to vent our frustrations and turn petition into progress. There are forces in place that want to rule the planet and all of its precious resources, we are disposable players in their sick, sick game; Monopoly in real life. We have given our power away – stop letting shiny shit impress you!

We have bought into their plan hook, line and sinker. After years of gratuitous conditioning and mass lack of independent thought we have become sheep who have ultimately been led to the slaughterhouse. Please do not accept my words as an indictment on the poor; Jesus noted that the poor will always be among us. But somewhere along the line it became too easy to not pay attention to matters of importance.

66 *I freed a thousand slaves. I could have freed a thousand more if only they knew they were slaves.* **99**

– Harriet Tubman

2

How Schools, Church, Media, Government and Other Institutions Failed Us

An insincere and evil friend is more to be feared than a wild beast; a wild beast may wound your body, but an evil friend will wound your mind.
Buddha

What happened to our social promise? We do what we're supposed to do and they do what they're supposed to do and life is well in Mayberry. The answer, my friend, is a simple one. We have been duped, hoodwinked, led-astray and bamboozled in large measure because we were asleep and they knew it. The institutions we trusted understood that we were not asking the right questions and took advantage of us.

When my younger son was in elementary school and found himself in hot water and under scrutiny from my husband and me he'd never quite answer the question we asked him. He'd give us an answer totally unrelated to the question and dance around the issue until it was almost funny. After imposing a plausible punishment we'd retreat to our bedroom and ask each other, "Does he really think we are that stupid?" I recently asked him if he left any dishes in the sink and he responded, "Daddy went to the store," we laughed in unison. After the laughter subsided I asked him again, "Are there any dishes in the sink?"

"No, mom."

"Okay, thanks, just make sure you clean up your mess."

Our smiles and laughter notwithstanding, I still needed an answer to my question; and he obliged. Now if our leaders could only do the same.

Below, I have provided the results from several polls asking if America is going in the right direction or is on the wrong track; as you can see by the numbers, overwhelmingly almost two thirds of respondents believe America is on the wrong track.

Direction of the Country
April 2012
Source: www.realclearpolitics.com/polls

Poll	Date	Right Direction	Wrong Track	Spread
RCP Average	4/5-4/17	31.8	61.8	-30.0
NBC News/Wall St. Jrnl	4/13-4/17	33	59	-26
CBS News/NY Times	4/13-4/17	31	61	-30
Reuters/Ipsos	4/12-4/15	35	60	-25
Rasmussen Reports	4/9-4/15	27	65	-38
ABC News/Wash Post	4/5-4/8	33	64	-31

Our America was built on a reciprocal trust system. Real work was available right after high school, and a job for life was guaranteed so long as we arrived on time, didn't steal company time and performed to their best of our ability. If we decided to attend college, then hey, we'd have more choices and a better chance to really excel in life. In turn companies rewarded loyal employees with health and life insurance, pay raises and an opportunity to excel based on merit. In my case, like many other women, I graduated from college and opted to stay at home and raise my two sons. I trusted my husband to provide for us so I could maintain our home. In Mayberry the trust cycle was simple; in Manhattan the trust cycle is much more complex. When consumers lose confidence about the stability of their income it affects their spending activity and ultimately compromises the national economy.

My older son attended seven schools in twelve years, not because anything was wrong with him, but because I perpetually believed he was not being challenged or prepared for life after the 12th grade. He attended parochial school until 3rd grade; at that point his school experience began to include more religious doctrine and since we weren't even catholic I knew it was time to pull him out. We found a great private school for 4th grade but once we learned there would be no tuition break for siblings I was tasked with finding a suitable school once he hit 5th grade and my younger son started kindergarten the following year.

During my search I saw a small ad in our local paper advertising openings for a charter school – a new type of public school that features smaller class sizes, longer school days, a longer school year and uniforms. Since private school tuition for two children was not viable at the time we opted for the charter school with cautious expectations. The ad said I had to write a letter, postmarked by the deadline, to request an application; upon receipt of the application I had to send it back fully completed by another deadline. Once they received my application, they would send me a letter in the mail advising if my children had been accepted into the school; if they were not accepted for capacity reasons, they would be placed on a waiting list until slots opened for them. All I could do was pray that they were both accepted so I wouldn't have to drive one kid to one school and the other to another – what a nightmare that would be in the middle of a New York snowstorm. Thankfully, they were both accepted.

Charter schools are funded with public money (the government) but are run by a private board and are sometimes managed by for-profit management companies, as was the case with my children's school. The final step to their acceptance into the school was the submission of their transcripts from our local public school. Well, in my older son's case he was transferring from a private school and in my younger son's case this would be his first time attending school so I was unable to provide that last piece of documentation. Since the school needed those records, I was forced to register both of my children in our local public school then transfer them right back out and provide the charter school with such. I can only assume for "billing purposes" the state needed some verification that my children actually existed before they would release payment to the new school for my children's education.

The charter school was brand new and operating out of trailers but I didn't care; neither did all of the other parents who pulled their children out of private, parochial, and Montessori schools for this cost-effective learning module. As I began networking with other parents I soon realized we all shared the same hopes and desires for our children's future. We were smart and educated and worked closely with the school to ensure our children received the world-class education the ad promised us.

After year one, the school was ready to move out of the trailers and into their brand new building. Test scores were high, the children were learning and things appeared to be going well. At the start of the second year of operation, I was invited to sit on their board of trustees and I gladly accepted the invitation. As a board member I became privy to how charter schools actually run, I believed in the movement and was happy to be involved. Sadly, this would be my older son's last year there; the school stopped at 6th grade and I was now, again, charged with finding him school; this time a feeder middle school to a great high school.

One evening, as I was pouring through financial statements and academic reports, I realized our school was not being totally upfront with our public reporting. Let me be clear, the numbers were **never** manipulated while I was a board member but the narrative was not one hundred percent. Our school publicly touted our excellent standardized testing scores, what we didn't share publicly was the challenging enrollment process. See, the admission process alone was enough to weed out a particular type of family/socioeconomic type. Only parents who were willing and patient enough to carefully read, understand and act accordingly to the multi-tiered directions and applicable deadlines would be privileged enough to have their children admitted into this new type of public school. The process alone guaranteed students from higher income earning families with strong academic backgrounds. Great test scores during the first two years of operation could not possibly be credited, in totality, to the school; especially since it was a brand new academic model. The reporting was disingenuous at best. Once the word got out that the students were excelling head and shoulders above their traditional school counterparts parents engaged in a feeding frenzy to get their kids in.

I never lost faith in the charter school movement, as a whole, so we enrolled my older son into a charter middle school for 7th and 8th grades while our younger son stayed in the new elementary charter school.

The summer of 2001, two weeks before 9/11, we purchased our dream home in Atlanta. We chose our home, as most parents do, based on the school system. Our older son enrolled in an awesome public high school and our younger son started 3rd grade at a charter school in our area. After a few years in Atlanta, we moved back to the New York. My older son graduated from our local public high school and our younger son attended a charter middle school and went on to graduate from our local public high school. After all has been said and done...I want a refund!

The government has paid, best guess, $210,000 ($5^{th}$-$12^{th}$ = 8 years x $10k + K-$12^{th}$ = 13 years x $10k) to educate my children and sans my obsession for educational excellence they would never have been prepared for life after 12th grade. This is inexplicable for a developed country like ours. Parents should be outraged and protesting in the streets that education costs so much in this country; yet can't trust that a job will be there, regardless of a college degree, for their children. What are we paying for? And why can't we trust the educational system in this country to educate our children, even at the lowest level, to marginally survive.

If you don't believe me...peep this; I purchased groceries not too long ago and the bill was $12.36 – I gave the young lady $13.00 as I was still reaching for change in my purse. She entered $13.00 in the register as I was handing her .11 cents more. She asked me what I was giving her the .11 cents for as she was handing me back .64 cents change. I told her I wanted three quarters back – she glanced at the register LED (which indicated $.64) then glanced back at me, and then glanced back at the register LED in a very puzzled way. It was my quick assessment that anyone working a cash register at a grocery store would be able to count and manage money quickly to keep the line moving. I love computers and smart phones and technology but they should be used to enhance our knowledge, not replace it.

While raising our children, we frequently attended weekly church service. By the time our older son was in high school I had written *From Hip-Hop to Heaven, From Hip-Hop to Heaven for Girls* and he served as the cover model for my 3rd book *Can Hip-Hop be Holy?* I was the Youth Director of our church and my husband was the Sunday School teacher for the boys in our congregation. As we rose in leadership we began to question our place in ministry. Our role was to be an example of God and light to others, not secure the long term financial stability of the church or serve as the de facto stop-gap for short term financial calamities. I've asked myself many times, "When did church become a business?" I thought church was about bonding with other believers; my former home church is now down to less than 100 members and the average age of the congregation is over 50 years old. Contemporary churches are lively, with-it and actively online, while older ones are holding onto religion; both with reckless abandon.

The Philadelphia Archdiocese has been under investigation for many years. In 2012 a defrocked priest plead guilty to sexually assaulting a 10 year old altar boy and was sentenced to 2½ to 5 years in prison. During the same year a monsignor was accused of covering up the priest's misdeeds along with a reverend who is accused, in the same investigation as the priest, of the attempted rape of another minor. The monsignor and the reverend have both plead not guilty and are awaiting trial as this book went to print. The most disheartening aspect of this scandal is that accused pedophiles were allowed to stay in ministry and were shuffled from parish to parish to lead the uninformed faithful. We have been plagued with story after story about priests having their way with impressionable young boys and girls. There is a trailer load of men, who for some reason or another, found it necessary to rob children of life and their lives. It's obvious the Catholic Church cannot self-regulate; I hope justice prevails for the sake of the victims.

When reporting on the scandals of the church, media outlets always lead with the most salacious attention-grabbing headline - priests having sex with little kids. There's a saying in the media, "If it bleeds it leads." No bias there, right? The media's purpose is to make money – it is a business. With the advances in technology over the past fifty years the influence of the media has grown exponentially. Sadly, we have become sheep who rely on Bain Capital/Thomas H. Lee Partners (Clear Channel), CBS Corporation, Gannett Co., Time Warner,

Inc., Tribune Company, Viacom, Walt Disney Company and Washington Post Co. for television and radio programming; AT&T, Cablevision Systems Corporation, CenturyLink, Charter Communications, Inc., Comcast Corporation, News Corp., Sprint Nextel Corporation, T-Mobile USA, Inc., Time Warner Cable, Inc. and Verizon for access to high speed Internet service; Bertelsman, Gannett Co., The Hearst Corporation, News Corp., Tribune Company and the Washington Post Co. for print news and Apple, Facebook, Google, Microsoft and Yahoo! for keeping us connected with our friends and co-workers through user-generated content and our social networks.

As a result of so many mergers, the above named companies control what news we receive and how we receive it. I started my radio show in 2008 to share news with my readers that they may not hear elsewhere – after my mom lost her battle with ovarian cancer in 2009 I took a hiatus; in my spirit I knew I had to get back on the air. I created a show that I would actually want to listen to every day. These corporations are not operated by the morality police; their job is to return a profit to their shareholders.

Politicians work in tandem with the media to influence public opinion; that's why they talk in sound bites (short clips extracted from a longer piece of audio). How can we trust people to fight for us if we don't have the patience to listen to them for more than five seconds? Lawmakers would argue that we don't want the truth – so they take the liberty to give us what they think we want to know – then use the media to deliver their content in a manner that we are most receptive to. Politicians need to know we are a lot smarter than they give us credit for.

Our institutions have failed us; schools, churches, media, our government and others. There is no easy answer to this dilemma, but if left unaddressed will get worsen very quickly. I taught my children to question authority (much to the chagrin of my grandmother), but my mom raised me to question authority and we typically parent the way we were parented. I was viewed by others as a very disrespectful child at times; I was just inquisitive and wanted to know the answers to questions adults may not have wanted to answer at the moment. My parenting techniques have come back to bite me in the butt several times, but I would do it all over again the same way. I did not raise sheep! I raised men who knew how to put a subject with a predicate and ask intellectual questions.

It's not too late to ask our institutions, "Why?" and ask them to make good on their end of the bargain. We played by the rules and so should they.

3

Mentally Working Your Way Through Unemployment

Problems are not stop signs, they are guidelines.
Robert H. Schuller

Many people are now faced with the harsh reality that their career is not as financially solid as they thought. In many instances the salary paid in exchange for a particular skill and work provided has not kept up with the times; in other instances the owners of the company they work for just don't want to pay cash + benefits + paid time off anymore. We live in a capitalistic society; employers are mandated to do what they must to positively impact their bottom line, frequently with little regard to employees' needs. Sadly, there is little legislation to compel company owners to play nice and fair with the "little people." There are laws in place to force companies to pay a minimum wage and to make them pay extra wages for overtime, but where are the laws to prevent jobs from being shipped overseas? There are none.

President Bill Clinton stated on December 8, 1993, in his remarks before the signing of the North Atlantic Free Trade Agreement (NAFTA), "We are on the verge of a global economic expansion that is sparked by the fact that the Unites States at this critical moment decided that we would compete, not retreat." That comment along with many eyebrow-raising others Clinton made in his speech that day were given just a few days after the birth of my second son so I was pretty out-of-the-loop on current events. I remember reading about the trade agreement and specifically his speech a few weeks later and feeling an instant knot in my stomach. The knot returned as I was reading *The Contract With America* by the Republican National Committee just a year later.

The North American Free Trade Agreement (NAFTA) is an agreement signed by the governments of Canada, Mexico, and the United States, creating a trilateral trade bloc in North America.

The flag representing the union of the United States, Mexico and Canada under NAFTA

The area in the world indicating the countries involved with NAFTA

A trade bloc is a type of intergovernmental agreement, often part of a regional intergovernmental organization, where barriers to trade, (tariffs and non-tariff barriers) are reduced or eliminated among the participating states. It superseded the Canada – United States Free Trade Agreement between the U.S. and Canada. In terms of combined Gross Domestic Product (GDP) of its members, as of 2010 the trade bloc is the largest in the world.

http://en.wikipedia.org/wiki/North_American_Free_Trade_Agreement

Implementation of NAFTA began on January 1, 1994 and removed most barriers to trade and investment among the United States, Canada, and Mexico. Under NAFTA, all non-tariff barriers to agricultural trade between the United States and Mexico were eliminated. In addition, many tariffs were eliminated immediately, with others being phased out over periods of five to fifteen years. This allowed for an orderly adjustment to free trade with Mexico, with full implementation beginning January 1, 2008. The agricultural provisions of the U.S.-Canada Free Trade Agreement, in effect since 1989, were incorporated into the NAFTA. Under these provisions, all tariffs affecting agricultural trade between the United States and Canada, with a few exceptions for items covered by tariff-rate quotas, were removed by January 1, 1998. In the years after NAFTA was passed,

http://www.fas.usda.gov/itp/policy/nafta/nafta.asp

The U.S. exported $248.2 billion in goods to Canada and $163.3 billion in goods to Mexico; the top two purchasers of US exports in 2010.

We purchased $276.4 billion in goods from Canada and $229.7 billion in goods from Mexico; the second and third largest suppliers of goods imports to the United States in 2010.

The U.S. goods trade deficit with NAFTA was $94.6 billion in 2010, a 36.4% increase ($25 billion) over 2009.

The U.S. goods trade deficit with NAFTA accounted for 26.8% of the overall U.S. goods trade deficit in 2010.

The U.S. had a services trade surplus of $28.3 billion with NAFTA countries in 2009 (the latest data available).

An increase in domestic manufacturing output and a proportionally greater domestic investment in manufacturing does not necessarily mean an increase in domestic manufacturing jobs. This increase may simply reflect greater automation and higher productivity; although the U.S. total civilian employment may have grown by almost 15 million in between 1993 and 2001, manufacturing jobs only increased by 476,000 in the same time period. Furthermore from 1994 to 2007, net manufacturing employment has declined by 3,654,000, and during this period several other free trade agreements have been concluded or expanded. This is partially to blame for job losses across many sectors affecting those who live and work in America.

What at one time might have been an unusual story has now become far too common in America. Many have lost their job, are worried that they may get laid off or know someone who is really going through. We are living in very tight times for those who don't have a job. I know it's tough getting on the Internet everyday looking for a job, sitting on perpetual hold with the unemployment office, and watching politicians debate jobless benefits extensions; stay encouraged and hold on, God has something for you. Nothing is ever as it seems, nor is it as bad as it looks at that moment. There is a way to work through the challenge of not having a job. Because of globalization, technology and the global economy, we have been forced to rethink how we do so many things.

On the train heading into New York City one morning I overheard two women talking, one of the women shared that as she and her co-workers sat down to begin their day a few of them could not gain access to their computers. So, they restarted the computers and checked all of the plugs but nothing was working. We all know what that can feel like – you just want to sit down, start your day and do what you have to do. They figured the IT department was working on something and decided to get some coffee hoping everything would be back to normal when they got back to their desks. As soon as they sat back down from their coffee run someone from Human Resources walked over to one of the women and asked, "Can you come with me?" She didn't think anything of it and obliged. A short time later she returned to her desk escorted by company security; she was given 20 minutes to clear her desk and leave the building. This same process, as I overheard the conversation, was repeated a few times that morning. I thought to myself, "what a way to start the day." This woman was let go from her company with no advance warning, no reasonable explanation and is now left to reset her life and lifestyle. This woman was penalized for something she didn't do – she played by the rules and was screwed. Is it fair to force the masses into a whirl-wind because profit margins are not up to shareholder expectations? If this has happened to you – do not let this situation become the story of your life. There is nothing wrong with you and you can get through this.

To anyone who has found themselves without a job...stop looking for a *job* and look for work.

Think beyond, "I need to get a job," your survival is contingent upon having multiple streams of income. Change your thinking from, "I'm going to work," to "I am working." There is a huge difference between the two; I don't go to a job, but I work, in every sense of the word, every single day as an author, media personality and keynote speaker. I have been self-employed for many years and my grandmother still asks me what should she tell people at church I do for a living. Sometimes she'll call me and I'll be right in the middle of something and I'll tell her,

"Grandma, I'm working can I call you back later?"

She'll say, "I'm sorry I thought you were at home."

"No grandma, I am at home but I am working."

"Huh."

"Never mind grandma, I'll call you back later."

You don't have to go to a job to earn a decent living for yourself and for your family. Use your down time to look for work and ways to guarantee multiple streams of income instead of seeking the increasingly elusive full-time career job with benefits and a pension. Your financial future depends on it. So many times we blow off people's dreams and side hustles; don't do that. We don't know their situation. A friend of mine had a great job and on the weekends sold t-shirts in Harlem with a host of other street vendors. When he lost his job the financial blow was cushioned by his side-hustle. He was able to pivot and keep it moving. He is now a very successful street vendor; everyone has a back story how they got there – we see them all the time – support them. Staying nimble in life is critical. Have you ever noticed how football players and basketball players and tennis players can be in mid-stride, yet are able to turn on a dime and totally change the game? You can do the same with your life. Don't get stuck. Stay nimble and flexible.

A job does not validate you; validation comes from peace knowing you can pay your bills and take care of your family.

Find a quiet place, take a deep breath and go inside for peace and solace. There is a direct correlation between a rise in unemployment and suicide. In my living room I have this huge chair – it's almost the size of a love seat - and early in the morning I curl up in it and think. My family is still asleep, it's still dark outside and I spend this time talking with (not *to)* God and planning my life. Spending quiet time each morning allows me to reorganize the plans I discussed with God the morning prior. Life is full of constant adjustments and rearrangements; I am not easily shaken when things happen around me each day because, for the most part, God has already told me what is going to happen. It becomes easier to maneuver through life when you know what's going to happen. God gives us hints, signs and signals all of the time, but unless we are alert in the moment and aware of our surroundings we'll miss it. Your intuition is God speaking to you and if you're going – and going – and going your energy becomes too busy to receive signals and instructions. Slow down.

Use your private morning time to journal. Write down what you want in life, write down how you are feeling; don't worry about any spelling or grammatical errors. The key is getting these thoughts out of your head and onto paper. Write down all of the things you are thankful for, rewrite the list everyday if that's what you need to do. It could be as simple as the neighbor's dog didn't bark too loudly yesterday or that sharp pain in your side has subsided. Get inside of your own head; work *with* God to work through your feelings and emotions.

> Stop being angry and bitter when things happen to you, just accept that life is not always going to be rosy and sunny and keep it moving. The key is having a coping mechanism in place so you can quickly rebound.

It took me years to learn this lesson. Every time something happened to me that I didn't like or understand I'd retreat to my bed and stay there; sometimes for days on end. Really. Bed was my attempt at coping; which is not a practical way to handle life. Once I began spending time talking with God in the morning I felt more confident when challenges came my way; I had an armor bearer with me at all times. Life got better and the bed no longer became my place of refuge but a place to actually sleep at night.

I need you to understand that you are not a failure, what working looks like for most Americans has changed. Due to many factors, we did not properly prepare ourselves for what was to come. Don't stop working to make your career dreams come true no matter what.

4

Navigating A Career Change

He who rejects change is the architect of decay. The only human institution which rejects progress is the cemetery.
Harold Wilson

Finding yourself without a job, in the wrong job or in a dead end job is very sobering. All of your energy may have been channeled to something that isn't returning the love. It's okay; know that you are not alone. Changing the way that you think about your career and your life will give you a sizeable advantage over everyone that is still asleep. The way that you earn a living should make you happy. If you are not happy with your lifestyle then seriously consider doing something else. Changing your perspective will make you a better and stronger person that handles setbacks with ease.

My husband has enjoyed an awesome career since my children were young. He left the house for work most days by 6am and frequently returned home exhausted around 7pm but he loved what he did. I stayed at home and handled every aspect of our home life – soup to nuts. He never had to worry about anything on the home front because that was my job. After I graduated from college I started a side hustle promoting parties. During the day I'd work the phones (this is very prior to email, the Internet and cell phones) and get things in place; I'd pick the kids up from school, handle homework, dinner and prepare them for bed. On nights where I had an event I'd be ready to walk out the door as soon as he walked in and usually didn't return home until about three in the morning. After getting home very late one night from an awesome party I realized I left the sponsor's banner at the venue. Those banners are quite costly and I had to get it so I could return it to my sponsor. By the time I got home, for the second time that night, he was waiting by the door ready to leave for work not realizing that I had already been home and left back out. In the most sarcastic manner he said wryly, "Can you make it home at least before I have to leave for work?" And walked out the door slamming it behind him.

We didn't speak for the whole day (remember this was prior to cell phones) so I sat at the door ready to explain the case of the forgotten banner as soon as he arrived home that evening. Instead, he went on and on about how hard he works and how I'm running the streets and partying all night. That very second I heard the virtual record skip. The spirit of humility flew out the window and in rushed major attitude. All I could shout back was, "Don't be mad at me because you chose a boring career! My career *is* partying! I'm not out partying, I'm out working!" I stormed out the room and slammed the door. The next year or two was a tumultuous time in our marriage. No man, who has a traditional job, wants his wife out all times of the night regardless if the house is clean and the children are well kept. I knew I needed to change my career to save my family.

I slowed down the on-site promotions aspect of my career and with the growth of a new medium called the Internet began marketing parties online and developing promotional campaigns for my clients. Not only was it more lucrative but it quieted my schedule which made him happier. Many women may read my story and think I wasn't strong enough to fight for what I believed in, but the truth of the matter was that it was more important to keep him happy so I could stay home and raise my children than have a full-time career at that time. So I had to shift a few things and make it work for me.

Successfully navigating a career change takes careful planning and a resolve to win.

Instead of totally changing my career, I created a new role for myself with in the same industry. I evolved with the changing times and made it work for the benefit of my home, my family and myself. Any career change, however, involves deep personal exploration and resolve to do what is important to you, not what is expected of you.

Changing your career may involve going back to school or taking classes on how to improve your skills – if that's what you need to do go for it! Going to school to get a degree or another degree is something you can be proud of and will help you better monetize opportunities that may come your way. Sometimes we have to take a step down to take three steps up. When you reset your career you'll find greater happiness, additional resources and exude more confidence in the marketplace. Successfully using your God given talent guarantees you income for life!

If you're searching for a new job, don't give up. Never give up, there is something out there just for you.

Often people will slip into depression over the loss of a job, the loss of income and the inability to find a suitable replacement. Don't despair, there is something out there for you, just keep moving forward. If you find yourself searching for a job with no luck please don't worry, put your trust in God and keep moving forward. The bible says the wealth of the wicked is stored up for the righteous (Proverbs 13:22) and since God is not in the counterfeiting business trust that money will work its way to you. The same goes for your next job – it's out there; maybe it's in the process of being created just for you. Don't let your age or experience level keep you from an opportunity – don't count yourself out before the other side does. The few jobs I have had during my adult life were all created for me. It may take completing 101 applications before you receive a call from a prospective employer, so the more you put out, the greater your chances are for getting a call back.

Money is often the reason why many couples part or divorce. It's a serious challenge for families to work their way through long-term unemployment; the shift in financial responsibility may become burdensome. Sit down and talk with your family members and let them know how *you* are feeling – there may be bitterness and resentment from both sides but don't internalize the conversation. Put them in your memory bank and get back on your grind at the very next opportunity to do so.

Use every resource at your disposal.

Keep in mind there are many resources you'll want to use when changing careers. Of course temporary agencies are a great place to start, you may not get exactly what you're looking for but you may get something. The Internet is another great source for finding opportunities suitable to your background and your goals; the daily newspaper is still a very affordable medium used by potential employers to find employees, so don't overlook the morning paper. My all-time favorite vehicle for finding income generating opportunities is your contacts.

Make your contacts count.

I have personally seen many good opportunites lost because one person doesn't like another person for some reason. Really? When you're out in this world scrapping for your livlihood put your feelings aside and just get things done. Where there are people there are people problems but you can't let that stop you from making necessary career moves. When you object to working with someone you are, in essence, cutting yourself off from everyone who they are connected with as well. Can you afford that? Not in this economy I don't think you can. Your contacts are your best resource for changing your life either for the better or for worse.

A few years ago I was unable to pay my cell phone bill so I sent out an email asking some of my contacts for assistance. I put my pride aside and did what I had to do.

A few of my contacts thought the email was a joke but others knew I was serious. One man, whom I've never met, but was on my mailing list, sent me $50. He said I inspired him because I didn't let my pride get in the way when I needed help. Another of my friends called the cell phone company and put $100 on her credit card. My bill was only $162.00 and two people paid 90% of that in less than an hour. I had to go back online and tell people to stop sending me money. One lady mailed a $5.00 bill to my house with a note saying that was all she had but I could have it. I have financially recovered and paid bills for other people since that time but understand the power of your relationships and how your contacts can make you or break you.

Many people believe their job defines who they are, it doesn't. You define who you are based on your values, morals and your culture. Your job is something you do – your life is what you live. God knows how to turn things around instantly in your favor, you just have to believe. Don't be discouraged there is something out there for you; you just have to navigate the path and walk the journey to get it.

Virtual Money

Wealth is in ideas - not money.
Robert Collier

The disparity between the *haves* and the *have-nots* expands with each passing hour. The fallacy lies in the premise that the *haves* simply decided to do more with their lives and the *have-nots* simply haven't. That can't be further from the truth. I've spent more time in my adult life with the have-nots than with the haves, and my achievements in life cannot be attributed to my burning desire to win in life. Where I attended school, my mom's friends, my ability to speak well, my height, being a debutante in a cotillion, my long natural hair, and a host of other traits gave me an edge over others. These are childhood factors that shaped my thinking and whether directly or indirectly better positioned me in life. I made several missteps during my teen-age years, as most do, but because of my background I was able to rebound rather quickly. How does one rebound if success mechanisms and a support system are not in place?

My older son was born between my senior year of high school and my freshman year in college; my mom and stepfather paid my college tuition (but made me work a part-time job), helped me pay for an in-home caregiver for my son and kept me encouraged until I graduated. No matter how determined, another young mother from a different background probably would not have been able to thrive in life as I have been able to because we didn't start out at the same place. I had help...and a lot of it.

The have-nots have been wrongfully accused of making countless excuses for their inability to thrive; the accusers are those who have the power to remove the barriers to entry but refuse to do so because in so doing threatens their very way of life. My dad told me that his dad told him, "...the only difference between rich people and poor people is that rich people have time to think." My grandfather was so right! Those from poor communities are less likely to own their own vehicle thereby adding approximately 90 minutes or more to their daily routine. I can drive to my office from my home and be seated at my desk with coffee in under 40 minutes – when I take the bus I'm just at my first transfer at 40 minutes. The hustle and bustle that comes with trying to make a dollar out of fifteen cents leaves you tired, impatient for change, bitter, and in the long term doubtful about life ever changing. I have lived what I'm talking about. When you factor in diminished access to quality groceries, the prevalence of cheap fast foods and dilapidated housing one has to wonder how *does* someone escape poverty.

👍 Ask God for ideas, not money. Ideas and intellectual property are the new currency.

During the depression between 2008 and 2012 many people found it almost impossible to get a bank loan for things like a car or a home; being funded for a business venture was totally out of the question. This is great news to those from marginalized communities. In the past we didn't have a shot, now we do. We've had to fight to survive since day one; we now have an edge over those newly minted into our class. I started one of my most lucrative businesses to date with less than $300. It can be done!

👍 Turn your idea into a side hustle.

The financial meltdown under President George Bush and slow recovery under President Barack Obama was, in my opinion, the great equalizer. If someone had an idea and a little money they were in a sweet position to actually make something happen for themselves. Ideas and intellectual property are the new currency; things that can be traded for real dollars and a successful future. Treasure the thoughts that God gives you, use your ideas and accumulated wisdom to turn your situation around. Seek those who are where you want to be and partner with them. Use all of your gifts and skills to better your life.

Far too many times we are dismissive of peoples side hustle. My first business was a side hustle that gave me something to do while my children were in school and it turned out to be a real source of income for our family. Don't let the opinions of others take you off track. If God gives you an idea or a vision go for it. Fear will cause you to not take action and becoming bitter and angry about your fear will cause you to become stuck where you are. This may cause a vicious cycle in your life – don't get stuck. If you believe God wants more for you then that's all the faith you need.

Manifesting your ideas into something viable is the highest form of gratitude to the Creator.

👍 If you've found yourself without a job, use your ideas to allow God to feed you another way.

Many people have lost their jobs and primary source of income; use your ideas and relationships to allow God to feed you another way. We have been told that our existence is contingent upon going somewhere every day, performing a task and getting a check every seven or fourteen days – it's high time we understand that is not the only way to earn a living. Perhaps God is calling you to something higher. Don't be limited by your own beliefs. You are an awesome individual with so much to offer to the world. You are bigger than your circumstances – prove it to yourself!

Beloved, please get rid of your debt; pay it down or declare bankruptcy if you have to but living with an overload of debt will keep you thinking the old way – a job, a paycheck and bills. With reduced debt, you open yourself up to more opportunities in life – you can transfer to another city for an opportunity and you have the freedom to live life on your terms, not those bound by limited resources because you are saddled with debt.

See, when monetary transactions became relegated to plastic we became disillusioned about how much we were spending and what we were spending it on – this is part and parcel of the game that is being played on the masses. Plastic made every purchase okay. I was tricked and so were you. Virtual money is still money no matter what form you spend it in. Go online and check your credit card balances, and then set yourself up on a plan to pay off the cards that charge the highest interest rates first. If you can consolidate your debt to one or two cards with zero interest for a year or two take it! Do whatever you need to do – no matter how drastic – to rid yourself of debt. It is taking years always from your life. In most cases you're losing opportunities to better yourself because the decisions you're making are based upon your need for a job to pay your debt. Please learn to live within your means. If you don't have it to spend – don't spend it.

A friend of mine owns an awesome birthday party venue and she shared a story with me how one of the parents asked her to drastically lower her rates so her child could invite more kids to their party. When she shared the story with me I asked her why the parent didn't just tell the child that there is a limit to the number of children who could attend because they couldn't afford it. How can you be honest with your kids about money if you can't even be honest with yourself about money? Since when did a birthday party become a necessity? I felt badly for the parent; they have become so victimized by what society says they should do that they found it easier to ask others to make concessions because telling the child, "no" is not an option.

Set some good financial goals for yourself. If you can't handle developing a debt reduction plan on your own, consider getting professional help. Make sure your plan includes a solid savings component as well. Give yourself time. Taking smaller steps and dealing with money management tasks one at a time will be a great help. It probably took you years to accumulate your debt so give yourself equal measure to get out of it.

> You don't have to get it right, you just have to get it going.

Making major changes in how you manage money is never easy – but I know you can do it. Ridding yourself of debt, spending less and saving more is an art that can be mastered. Keep in mind you are not a failure. We live in a capitalistic society that is based on spending money as fast as you earn it – it is a trick that has fooled many. Don't get all worked up over money – money is not good or bad it just is. It exists to help us help others on our journey. Don't get stressed out about how much so-and-so has and what you don't have; it is a trick. Make the choice to no longer be fooled. Pay attention to your financial life not the financial lives of those on reality television. Their lives are based on money, money and more money not the things that bring true joy and pleasure in life like family and peace and a sustained and sustainable lifestyle. When you focus and nurture what you *do* have you will always have more; when you focus on what you don't have you will never have enough. Make the choice today to confidently use your ideas to change your life and lives of those around you.

Retirement and Homeownership

Choose a job you love,
and you will never have to work a day in your life.
Confucius

There are so many options you'll have to consider when it comes to retiring and none of them are easy. I believe retirement is your chance in life to earn a living doing what you love most, not stop working altogether. No longer can we work for 40 years, retire, receive a check from the government each month and expect to live happily ever after; that narrative was reshaped in the 70's and through the 80's. Privatization and deregulation during those years were the instigators of the global financial meltdown in 2008.

When I started my first real job in the early 90's I asked my grandmother if she received a pension; she looked at me as if I said something wrong. Number one, most black people don't ask questions like that of their elders, but I wanted to know; number two, she wanted to know why I wanted to know.

She told me, "yes" she received a pension; and I asked her, "For what?"

"What do you mean for what?"

"Well, why would a company continue to pay you even though you stopped working there so long ago?"

"Because."

"Because, why?" I asked.

"Because that's what companies used to do." She said.

"Wow, so you mean if I worked at a company for many years, they'd continue to pay me even though I don't work there anymore?"

"Yes, that's what they're supposed to do."

"Well, I have never heard of that."

"Saideh, you have worked; how do you not know about a pension?"

"I know about a pension from what I've read but companies now don't even mention a pension when they hire you."

She shook her head and we moved the conversation to what we were going to eat for Sunday dinner.

At some point companies decided it was no longer fiscally sound to offer a pension to employees, so they did away with that perk. Meanwhile, people were still seeking jobs that offered a pension because they were not privy to the "memo" that pensions were being phased out because of its economic burden to the shareholders' bottom line.

When you leave your destiny in the hands of others, particularly those who don't have your back, you leave yourself open and vulnerable. I'm disheartened because hard working American's bought into a system that changed the rules but never notified the players. How are we supposed to win if we're playing one game and they're playing another? There is only one answer...pay attention to your surroundings. Everyone who suffered a loss during the economic meltdown must face the reality that their retirement, as they believe it should be, is in doubt. Remain cognizant of trends; do research on your own; listen to the conversation outside of your area code. Confidently know what is on the hearts and minds of the nation; that is your right and your responsibility.

👍 Homeownership is debt.

My grandmother and grandfather bought their home early in their professional careers; they worked for many years at the same job and by the time they retired it was paid for. That will never be the story for my husband and I, or many others whose chances of staying at one job for more than five years is slim to none. They had a shot at life based on the reciprocal promises between people and institutions. Buying their own home tied them to a neighborhood, it allowed them to plant roots; roots that were watered and cultivated and supported by local schools, churches, banks and the government. Those institutions gave us their ass to kiss and subsequent generations have been forced to take care of our basic needs – food – clothing – shelter the best way we know how. Times have changed; it won't benefit you or your family to hold onto old ways of thinking. What worked for my grandparents, who were born in the early 20's, will not work for us.

The beauty of homeownership ties you to a community while at the same time homeownership ties you to a community. We live in a global society right now and it's becoming more transient with each passing day. No one is able to truly plant roots anywhere anymore; and technically, why should we. A bohemian life has been forced upon us as a matter of survival. Perhaps those who live off the land are onto something. We owned a home for a few years and every penny we made was poured right back into it – no vacations, no eating out, nothing. When my husband was offered a job in a different state, we jumped at the opportunity to sell our home and move on with our lives. Now, as elusive as job offers are, homeowners may not be able to seize an opening as quickly if they're offered better employment outside of their immediate area because the housing market is so depressed. I am not rebuking homeownership forever but it should not be viewed as a financial guarantee for retirement or income. People who bought homes are finding that their homes are worth, in some cases, less than half of what they paid for it or still owe on it. That is not a sound investment by any stretch of the imagination and the lenders knew it.

Don't let old ways of thinking hinder your growth and mobility. We all want to have the best in life although it is not always easy to attain. I'm grateful my children were able to experience my grandparents' way of living – Sunday dinners, a front and back porch and a few gifts on holidays; I hope they weave those memories into the fabric of our world's new way of living to build a well-rounded future for their families.

7

It's Never Too Late To Succeed!

Don't judge each day by the harvest you reap
but by the seeds that you plant.
Robert Louis Stevenson

Estelle Scher, better known to us as Estelle Getty
was born in New York City in 1923 to immigrant parents
from Poland. She launched her career in Yiddish theater at
a time when women were systematically sidelined to their
male counterparts, personally and professionally. She
penned *If I Knew Then What I Know Now...So What?* in
1988, in which she serves up her famous wisdom and
advice on everything from marriage and motherhood to
Hollywood and hypochondria. Employed by odd jobs while
raising her two sons and maintaing a marriage, she never
lost her passion for acting and managed to squeeze in
auditions and small roles during her mid-life years.

It wasn't until 1985 when she landed the role of
Sophia Petrillo on the hit TV show *Golden Girls,* at the age
of 62, that she became famous. Estelle is quoted as saying,
"After 50 years in the business, I am an overnight
success."

We lost our beloved Estelle in 2008 from Lewy
Body Dementia and we will always remember her as the
feisty grandmother we wished we had. And in all that
Estelle stood for and accomplished, it is noted in several

53

articles, that she couldn't even remember her cast mates in the years proceeding her death. I trust she savored her success while she still had her memory.

I can only wonder how Estelle felt all of those years making a living but not following her heart. I have felt that way many times during my life and I am sure you have too. Sometimes we have to do what we have to do, whether we like it or not. Don't put pressure on yourself to succeed today...your soul needs time to prepare for all that God has for you. Today is the day to tackle your feeling of failure.

As long as you're alive, you still have a fighting chance.

A month after I turned 40 years old, my youngest son graduated from high school. As we began planning his life I knew I needed to plan mine. My older son was 21 years old and thriving on his own and neither one of them needed me like they did before. I found myself caught unprepared like so many others. I never really planned for this moment. When my older son graduated from high school four years earlier I should have started making preparations then; but I talked myself into thinking my younger son really needed me to check his homework every night and drive him where he needed to go. A week after his graduation I realized I was spiraling into a state of depression and I fought it with everything I had. I thought my life was over once they began living their own; but in all actuality, that was my moment to start living.

👍 Accept how you feel and why.

Before I hit the reset button I had to accept my feelings but more importantly understand why I was feeling the way I was. I spent the first half of my life totally dedicated to my children. While they were young and I was in college times were pretty lean; I sacrificed a lot. Once I graduated from college, things got a lot better. I started my own business and my children were with me in every sense of the word. I frequently adjusted my schedule based on theirs and they did the same for me from time to time. When they were sick, I felt liberated that I didn't have to ask my boss for a day off to care for them. The cost of this freedom wasn't free, however. It cost me current and future earnings because I was never able to monitarily maximize my professional skills because of my self-imposed over-commitment to my children.

I knew exactly why I felt a little resentment towards my children once they both graduated from high school but was it their fault? Of course not. Nor was it mine or my husband's. I knew I couldn't live the rest of my life bitter and angry at these two precious angels – they didn't ask to be here and they certainly didn't ask me to not work a "real job" so I could spend plenty of time with them. Those were my decisions; I put my big girl panties on and got over it. I was able to distinguish and clarify every aspect of how I was feeling. I needed to in order for me to move forward on my journey. God was not going to bring more into my life while I was holding onto feelings of rejection and abandonment from my children that were genuinely unfounded.

👍 Talk with as many people as you can who share the same challenges as you.

I struck up conversations at the grocery store, on the bus, the hair salon and anyplace I could to connect with moms who I believed felt like I was feeling at the time. I discovered 40 year old moms of toddlers who felt the same way I did; it wasn't about our age or the age of our children – it was really about dealing with a major change in our lives and how to effectively work through it. Talking with others was a great way for me to overcome my fear and anxiety about the future. I expressed my feelings with those I knew would understand to prevent me from saying something to my children I might regret later.

👍 Create a workable plan.

What kept me sane through those first few difficut weeks of empty-nesting, was assurance that *this too shall pass*. I know in good times and in difficult times we are all just going through. A few years down the road we may not even remember why we were feeling some kind of way and why we got so worked up. Sharing your feelings and getting help to create a plan for your life can make you feel better and offer a sense of purpose and direction. When you fail to plan, you certainly plan to fail.

👍 Rock your plan.

Don't allow yourself to self destruct before you can get your plan off the ground. Life has so much to offer you and you have so much to give; there is nothing you can't accomplish. Once your plan is in place you'll notice how feelings of failure will come and go, that's natural. Just don't get stuck when they come. Getting on with life and successfully executing your plan is something that you can definitely feel good about.

Understand that success is a journey, not a destination.

My children are thriving in the environments they created for themselves. They are astute, aware, grounded individuals who think for themselves and are aptly prepared to live with the outcomes from their decisions. I have done my job! I am not the only person on the planet to hit the reset button at age 40. Very often people do not give themselves the enough credit. You'll find that not only are you successful on some level, but you are worth more than you think. It's all about self-image and how you feel about yourself.

Many people don't think they're successful or valuable, but when you see your life through the eyes of others, I'm sure you'll find you're much better off than you thought. The grass may be greener on the other side of the fence but I bet their water bill is higher too. Success is truly in the eye of the beholder. You can experience success on so many different levels.

Frequent job changes were once viewed as a detriment on a resume to a potential employer; for the employee, however, they can reflect on the many friendships and relationships and laughter that has come from those work experiences.

Parents and spouses should view their success through the eyes of God; I was able to create a profound and lasting change in the lives of those who matter to me the most, my children. Do you have a kind heart? Are you envied by many because you have a lot of friends? If so, that makes you successful. You will find that with a kind heart, you'll be envied by many. A lot of people don't have it in them to be naturally generous. This is why not everyone volunteers their time or talents. Some people have a natural character trait that allows them to think about others without even considering themselves. While many people will take the time to consider other people, a quick thought of how they will be affected causes them to retreat.

I haven't mentioned money as a factor for success on any level for good reason. Money should never be the only or the key measure of success in life. What good is it for you to gain the whole world yet lose your soul (mind, will and emotions)? (Mark 8:36). You brought nothing into this world and you can't take anything with you when you depart from it (1 Timothy 6:7). Right now, society can be blamed for most of the things that are wrong with the world, but society is made up of people. People are the ones pressuring others to be perfect; to earn more, to do more, to make more. You can't control everything that happens to you or around you. On your journey you'll meet all kinds of people and where there are people, there are people problems. Don't lose who you really are trying to be perfect for someone else. Everyone is unhappy with some part of themselves (job, personal relationships, family, etc.), but if you're able to appreciate the things that you have, then you are a successful person. Keep in mind that no good deed goes unreturned. If you work hard for the things that you desire, you'll receive them. You get *from* the world what you *give* the world.

What successful living looks like to me

_____

_____

_____

_____

_____

_____

_____

_____

_____

_____

_____

LIFE REMIXED

Section
Two

✠

Knowledge
of Self

LIFE REMIXED

8

Knowledge of Self

Getting in touch with your true self must be your first priority.
Tom Hopkins

"Know thyself," is an aphorism that traces back to Ancient Greece and serves as a foundational tenet for those on the journey of personal development and spiritual oneness. Its simplicity is embraced by members of various religious groups as well as those who believe in no religion at all. Our new world glamorizes the "personalities" on reality television – but more often than not, we're captivated by the persona they've created not who they really are once the cameras are turned off. They become trapped in their caricature and risk losing fame and money if they try to reclaim their soul. Knowledge of self is about learning what makes you tick – what things move you and what your non-negotiables are. Those who are truly themselves have found a way to earn a decent living and maintain their self respect; a la Oprah.

I was told many years ago, because of my low self-image and desire to take my life on more than one occasion, that I needed to love myself. I always asked, "What for?" I saw no need to love myself because I never felt worthy of adoration; the story I told myself was that of guilt and shame because, in my head, I failed to live up to the standards my parents set for me. And since I didn't live up to those standards I must be a failure. I shot for the moon, hit a star and I still thought I failed; all before I was 25 years old. I had my whole life ahead of me and I couldn't even see it.

I spent many days and nights crying in my bed wanting life to be better but a wet pillow and a dream does not a good life make. With the encouragement of those closest to me I managed to get myself out of the bed and reset my life. It was one of the most difficult things I have ever had to do.

Listen to your body and pay attention to your health.

Good health is not a matter of luck; good overall health is conscious choice to age well. I understand how challenging access to quality care can be but I can't stress enough how important it is to visit your primary care physician at least once a year along with regular visits to the dentist. Some time ago I became negligent about my oral care, as a result I almost lost one of my back teeth. The nerve became exposed and it was too painful to even chew the most tender foods. I would chew what I could on the other side of my mouth and swallow as quickly as I could. I found myself swallowing huge chunks of food which disrupted my digestive system. Our bodies don't live in a vacuum; each part of our boy needs another part to function properly.

As a result of my dental emergency my children became more cognizant about proper dental care. I have always been maniacal about their overall health but once they saw first-hand the effects of my neglect the preachy moments have been few and far between.

Cultivate pure self love.

Every saint has a past and every sinner has a future so no matter where you are on your journey you must love yourself. Learn to love the essence of who you are, not just what you look like; I know a lot of pretty but mean people. Stand in front of a mirror totally naked and do it as often as you need to. Look at your face in the mirror - look at your pores, the color of your eyes, and the shape of your lips. If you really want to love yourself you must relinquish your insecurities and let go of your perceived flaws. Boldly present yourself to the world.

There are many things I'd like to do to my appearance but only as enhancements to my beauty not to make me beautiful. I'd love to lose weight - I can fix that. I'd love straight teeth - I can fix that. I'd love to go back to blonde hair - I can fix that. My current weight, teeth position and hair color are things that I can change to enhance how I present Saideh to the world; I am not going to hold off on presenting the world with my gifts and talents because I'm not skinny enough, or because my teeth are uneven or my hair is the wrong color. That's utter nonsense.

Whatever you feed will grow - if you feed yourself self-hatred then self-hatred will grow and take over your life, and maybe kill you. If you feed yourself love, and honesty and positive thoughts then that's what will grow in your spirit. We are all spirits mastering a human experience, so matters of the spirit are all that really matter. If you think I'm kidding talk to someone who has faced a near-death experience; they have the brightest disposition and outlook on life – regardless of what condition their body may be in.

The day we took my mother to the hospital for chemo they told her that they couldn't give it to her anymore because they didn't think it would help much; my mother looked at the nurse, smiled and asked, "How much time do I have?" She never stopped smiling; she transitioned five days later. When you love yourself as God loves us there is nothing in this world you can't handle. You can handle it and then some. Let go of your physical concern and deal with matters of the heart. It's okay to bare yourself to the world, we're all human. Use your insecurities as a filter, but never allow them to take control over your life.

👍 Embrace the world as your classroom

My older son began walking on his own by the time he was 11 months old and was talking soon after; my younger was trying to walk to keep up with his older brother by the time he was 9 months old. Although my younger son is 4½ years behind his brother he never let time, distance or age stop him from learning from his older brother and keeping up with him. My home became a classroom for me to teach my children life lessons and help them grow into responsible adults. I'd like to believe they learned just as much from me as they did from their teachers. Learning should never be relegated to a classroom; learning takes place right where you are right now. The overall system we've been duped into believing positions classroom instruction under the direction of a vetted authority as the single most important and authentic learning environment. It is under this system that fortunate students are awarded a certificate of completion indicating "X" number of years of study and are now qualified to be somebody (even if that somebody is not truly who they are or want to be). I believed in that system until I met countless people from that system who can't think for themselves.

"Then what did you go to school for?" I thought. If the premise of obtaining a degree was to get a better job, then why were college graduates not shielded from massive job losses – they, if anybody, should have been protected.

The world is your classroom, whether you're college educated or not wake up every morning and ask God to reveal something to you that you never knew before. Learning takes place wherever you are. Don't be fooled or led to believe that you are less-than because you don't have a college degree.

Many blue collar workers net the same, if not more, than white collar professionals. Blue collar workers are not expected to drive expensive cars nor are they expected to sustain an extravagant lifestyle – dollar for dollar they're probably more grounded and will be better off financially in the long run. My grandmother used to tell me, "You can learn a lot from a rock." Learn wherever you can; be open and receptive to every sign, message and smoke signal God sends your way; it's all for your greatest good.

👍 True wealth is experienceing success in all areas
   of your life.

Chris Rock once joked that a basketball player is
rich but the guy who signs his check is *wealthy.* His bit is
hysterically funny but only partly accurate; true wealth is
the result of being successful in every area of your life. You
can be successful in every area of your life if you choose to
be; 10% of life is what happens to you, the other 90% is
how you respond to it.

Human wants and needs are infinite; there will
always be desires to thrive and new areas to explore. When
EZPass and ExpressPay toll lanes were installed on
highways many complained about the loss of toll-taker
jobs; on the other side of that coin new jobs were created
as a direct result of the new programs operations. When
the vast majority of the workforce was in agriculture, it was
impossible to imagine what all those people would do if
they didn't have agricultural jobs. Then a hundred years
later the vast majority of the workforce was in industrial
jobs; again, it was impossible to imagine what workers
would do without those jobs. Now the majority are in
information jobs. If the computers get smart enough, then
what? I'll tell you: the *then what* is whatever we invent
next.

Respect the things you can't change
and take action for things that you can change.
Inspired by Milton Friedman

Everything Is Thought

Believe you can and you're halfway there.
Theodore Roosevelt

The world in which we live is radically different than the world we grew up in and the world we thought we'd inherit. We're all dealing with challenges that we aren't so aptly prepared for. Don't fret! You can do it. The challenges you may be facing are but mere transitional points on your journey. You are more prepared to deal with life right now than you think. Remain hopeful because things will change. That's nature. If you don't like cold weather, wait a few months it will be warm again.

The Law of Inertia states, "Something in motion tends to stay in motion and something at rest tends to stay at rest unless acted upon by an outside force." You give your life movement and stillness by your thoughts. The outside force in your life is your God-consciousness. At the core of this law is the notion that movement and stillness are constant and unchanging either in movement or stillness; unless something happens. Change takes place when something happens and the same is true in your life. Your life is still until your thoughts make something different happen. Everything changes but how you view change determines if things are changing for the better or for worse. Perception is everything.

Everything is thought; all of our energy and all of our intentions drive our thoughts.

Our life is the manifestation of the spiritual energy behind our thoughts and ideas; which drives the will to manifest our human intentions and leads to our actions that others see and shape their perception of us by.

Everything that happens in our life was a thought first – some thoughts are long and some are milliseconds – our thoughts are so powerful and are really the driving force in our lives. Our thoughts and our actions are mutually self-serving and work in partnership with each other. The energy behind our thoughts forces us to take a particular action and our future thoughts will now change as a result of the action taken.

Sometimes our thoughts may work on our behalf in an unfortunate way. I have personally witnessed someone constantly mumbling and grumbling about their job only to find they're unemployed a short time later. The Universe doesn't decipher your thought or intentions... if you constantly think, say and take actions against the furtherance of your current job then the Universe will oblige and remove you from the environment you think, say and act like you don't want to be in. Conversely, those who may come from a marginalized environment but think, talk and act successfully will look up on day and realized they have actually changed the trajectory of their lives and landed right where they wanted to be. The believe-achieve mantra may seem questionable to you based on your past experiences, your culture, your religious beliefs and the beliefs of your family and your friends but it's anchored in spiritual truth. We are spirits mastering a human experience so the essence of who we are operates on spiritual principles and laws not our five senses.

> Life is 10% what happens to you and 90% how you respond to any given situation.

When life gives you lemons, make lemonade because life can dish out some very sour situations. The last time I bit into a lemon it was pretty darn sour, but if I add some water and pour in a little sugar then stir it up a bit and put it on ice, after a short time in the refrigerator, I'll be able to sip something that I cannot just ingest but thoroughly enjoy. The way you think about a situation and how you ultimately handle it dictates how you grow and develop on your journey.

Horace Greeley is often credited with the famous quote, "Go west young man," actually said by John B. L. Soule. The quote first appeared as the title to the 1851, *Terre Haute Express* editorial written by Mr. Soule. Along with being wrongly credited to Mr. Greeley, it has also often been misquoted. It was originally written as "Go west, young man, and grow up with the country."

Our expansion westward was an exciting time in history. There was opportunity and adventure to be had for the young, unattached men of the time. There was also a great need for able bodied young men to help our young country forge a path through the wilderness of the untamed West. So, in great numbers they headed west to build another pillar in the foundation upon which our great nation now stands. Fast forward to today - often during times of our personal and professional quest for expansion we miss a turn and end up on a dirt road leading into the wilderness. Expansion is always exciting - with all of the newness and heightened expectancy, but sometimes our zeal takes us down the wrong path. "Go west young man," was a firm mandate; it was clear and concise and frequently that's how God gives us directions but because of outside stimuli we can't hear clearly.

I have shared many times publicly that I sometimes hear from God via clear, short, audible messages delivered into my left ear. I've cleared a lot of clutter and junk from my life because I don't want special messages delayed or blocked on its way to me. In so doing, my life has gotten better and better with each passing moment. Ironically, the more I place my intentions on clearing out clutter the more clutter and nonsense removes itself from my purview.

As I mature spiritually, I have become much more confident in listening, understanding and following my cues. Whether the message is "Go west young man," or "Give that lady a dollar," or "Be still," I know that everything is happening for my greatest good. Our thoughts are our power - the more our thoughts stay fixed on the Lord the more internal strength we have.

As the head goes, so does the body; where are the thoughts in your head leading your body?

Elderly people don't like to be alone so sometimes they intrude upon the lives of younger family members as a matter of their own comfort and survival. Over time their concerns are dismissed, conversations are shortened and one-on-one time becomes scarce. The very thing they feared – being alone – has come upon them based on their thoughts and actions.

As I've gotten older weight has become a bit of an issue with me, many women begin putting on a few more pounds in their 30's and it's not as easy to get off the older you get. I kept thinking was, "I don't want to be fat, I don't want to be fat," and the more I thought about not wanting to be fat the more weight I gained. My thoughts were grounded in lack and fear. I was subconsciously telling myself that anything in my life was permissible as long as I wasn't fat. As a result I ate more and was reckless with my body as long as I didn't reach fat weight – whatever that meant in my head. My thoughts should have been focused on being healthy; "I want to be healthy, I want to live a healthy life, I want wellness in my life." Operating from that point would have shifted my perspective from what I didn't want to what I truly wanted. When I thought about not being fat what I was really saying to myself was that I wanted to look good and feel good and that's what my thoughts should have been focused on. Once I changed my thinking about my health and appearance I began working out, eating better and feeling stronger; as a result (of the renewal of my mind) I have lost weight. Everything is thought and how we perceive life events determines the level of success we enjoy on our journey.

It's imperative you control your thoughts.

Where ever you place your thoughts your body will follow. You are a spiritual being that possesses a soul (mind – will – emotions) and lives in a body. Your spirit, by nature, is eternal and operates on spiritual principles while your soul is carnally driven and looks to the five senses for direction; mental anguish and conflict arise when the two don't agree on what the body should do next. Our thoughts ebb and flow hundreds of times a day and some negative thoughts may come upon us when we least expect it but the key is not staying fixated on them. Let them come in, and as easily as they come in...release them back to the nothingness from whence they came.

As children, many of us were given direction from our parents or other trusted elders, "do this," "don't do that," "sit here," "stop making so much noise," and the like; but what happens when we become grownups and those who provided direction are no longer around? We have become trained do-ers and not trained thinkers. I raised my children as thinkers and have been accused of having very disrespectful children (by those much older than I) because they talk back. My children are not rude but were perceived by some that, against our cultural norms, questioned me too much. If I raised my boys as do-ers and not thinkers how could they effectively advocate for themselves once I was no longer around? Sure, there were some pretty embarrassing moments when they flexed their intellectual muscle at inappropriate times, but I'd do it all over again the same way if I had to. Since our thoughts control our lives, why then do we not cultivate and train our youth to think? If we didn't, they would find themselves as adults lost and unable to process compound ideas and life's other complexities.

Our thoughts and the thought process are treasured gems and should be treated as such. Don't be a sheep and follow for the sake of following, train your thoughts to what is good and righteous and pure. You are what you think. Our thoughts are so powerful and yet thinking is often dismissed in our society as wasting time. It's not! The fast paced world in which we live is not a conducive environment to quiet thought – everybody is so busy doing that adequate time is not given to, "Am I doing the right thing," or "What am I doing this for?"

Live your life to the fullest each day, don't let fear or negative thoughts cause you to pass up a good thing. If you've always wanted to try something new get out there and work on it! Think about the things that make you feel good about yourself and what you have wanted to try for a long time. If you get out there and use your abilities to make your dreams happen you'll be happier and feel better about yourself.

The lives we lead are based upon the decisions we make and the decisions we make are based upon the thoughts we have *and* accept as real.

It's very difficult to see the light when you're in a dark place. A lot of people, especially in times of immense pressure, find themselves feeling hopeless – there's no time to feel hopeless. You're wasting precious moments feeling sorry for yourself. Look at the glass half full and not half empty. To truly change your life you're going to have to learn how to replace your negative thoughts and the perceived negative aspects of your life with positive ones, it's the only way. When things go wrong in your life, and they will, know that everything happens for our greatest good.

Three good thoughts I can bring into my spirit whenever I start to think negatively are...

_____

_____

_____

_____

_____

_____

_____

_____

_____

_____

Forgiveness and Self Sabotage

An insincere and evil friend is more to be feared than a
wild beast; a wild beast may wound your body, but an evil
friend will wound your mind.
Buddha

Christianity, Islam, Judaism, Hinduism and
Buddhism all teach forgiveness in a way that is meaningful
to their followers. I believe forgiveness is a gift we give
ourselves to free us from the past and help us move
forward in a more meaningful way on our journey. Peter
asks Jesus in Matthew 18:21-22,

"Lord, how many times may my brother sin against
me and I forgive him and let it go? [As many as] up to
seven times?

Jesus answered him, "I tell you, not up to seven
times, but seventy times seven!"

70 times 7 is 490, and that's a lot of forgiving!
There are people who have angered me and it took all I
had to forgive them; until I understood that forgiveness is
designed for me – not the person I'm angry with. Those in
need of forgiveness have probably moved on with their
lives and are on to bigger and better things while those
like me and others who have been wronged are angry,
bitter and turning our bodies into a powder keg waiting to
explode.

There are people I've had to forgive and have learned in later conversations with some of these people they didn't even realize how badly they made me feel. The spirit of forgiveness is born from a lack of understanding between the parties involved. When the need arises for you to forgive to help you live in the light and evolve, remember a few things:

👍 Forgiveness is not about condoning reckless or bad behavior from the others involved, its about cleansing your soul (mind–will–emotions) of the pain they left behind.

👍 Forgive in a way that works for you. There is no right or wrong way to forgive. If you need to cry – do it! If you need to go into a dark room and curse and scream – do it! If you need to pray or fast – do it! Do whatever you need to do, without bringing harm to yourself (drugs, food and other addictions included) to bring your spirit back into love and light.

👍 Don't sabotage your journey. Forgiveness includes letting go of your self-imposed feelings of rejection, inferiority, guilt, shame, neglect and any other feeling that keeps you from the light.

Forgiveness is not *your* mea culpa; it's an intentional space you reside in to be open and receptive to all the good that may come your way.

How To Be More Spiritual

You cannot believe in God until you believe in yourself.
Swami Vivekananda

Your spiritual journey starts by looking inward; there is no way to *become* spiritual – you *are* spiritual. We are all spirits, who possess a soul (mind-will-emotions) and reside in a fleshly body. There is nothing to become – spirituality is a presence that you're made aware of and chose to partake in as a lifestyle.

When I pulled out of the dealership in my first Honda Accord years ago, you know what I noticed....Honda Accords. These same Honda's would have been on the road next to me and in front of me but because of my heightened awareness and sensitivity to the brand and model they seemingly appeared everywhere. The same is true for many ideals that we adopt into our lifestyle. As soon as we become aware, we become aware.

Believe in something bigger than yourself; it's a matter of survival.

Your ego would have you belive *you're* the highest elevation and that *you* are the key to the sun rising and setting each day; that is not the case. There is a much bigger force in operation and until you regognize that God is at the helm you will continue to repeat painful lessons on your journey. Life is bigger than you; the evolution of humanity is bigger than you. You're not the one who ensures birds eat everyday; God makes sure the trees still bloom and the flowers grow every year. There is nothing you can do to make the Earth rotate – its all God. Your daily survival is contingent upon God's grace and mercy. God knows what you need before you can even ask – everything is right there for you all you have to do is believe.

👍 Stay fully present.

One of my favorite scenes in a film is from the movie *Hairspray* with Nikki Blonsky and John Travolta; in the scene Tracy Turnblad (Blonksy) tries to convince her "mom" Edna Turnblad (Travolta) to leave the house.

"Tracy, I haven't left this house in years."

"Isn't it time you did?"

"...I don't want to be seen like this. The neighbors haven't seen me since I was a size 10. Don't make me do it Tracy."

"Ma, it's changing out there, You'll like it! People are different, their time is coming."

The scene cuts and Tracy starts singing the song *Welcome To The 60's.* When you have time, please watch the movie, or at the very least the clip of the 6 minute scene on YouTube. During the song Edna realizes how much of her life she has missed out on from staying in the house because she thought she was too fat to go outside. By the end of the song Edna's hairstyle and clothes match the time period and she's dancing and singing with Tracy.

Edna put guilt on herself and missed out on so much. How much life are you missing out on because you feel some type of way about yourself? Let it go! Stay fully present in each moment. Look for life clues with every breath you take. God is there for you and offering direction to make your journey easier to navigate. Trust that there is something out there bigger than you, there is; and it's all for your greatest good.

> Spirituality is peace in your spirit that your conscious living is not eternally spent in survival mode; that your health and safety are taken care of so you can then care for others.

Spirituality is knowing we are one with God. God has given us the gift of free-will; and with this gift our liberties are endless. However, just because we can do something doesn't mean we should.

My spiritual journey started with a chance meeting with a friend and it took me ten long years to get to the place I needed to be to truly create a profound and lasting change in the lives of others. My ability to think freely cost me dearly. I should have shifted to God's way of doing things but I wanted to still do things Saideh's way. It wasn't working out for me...at all. I was afraid to walk boldly in my calling – I didn't want to be laughed at or mocked. I thought people wouldn't understand God the way I understood God. I should have held onto my Honda analogy. I didn't trust the universal system that was in place. The more I trusted the something-bigger-than-me premise the more I would have discovered people on the exact same journey as me. I tried to pour new wine into old wineskins and it took me ten years to figure out that my square peg wasn't going to fit into God's round hole.

The worst thing we as humans can do is mock something we don't understand; especially if what we're knocking is a projection of our self manifested in another human. When you knock someone else, you are realty knocking yourself because we are all an image of who we really are. We can morph ourselves into anything based on our thoughts – so when we criticize others we have stepped out of our spirit (the essence of who we are) and become a lower frequency version of our self. It is impossible to walk in the spirit realm and contentiously find the darkness in others. The only way for you to see the darkness in others is to become one with the darkness that resides in you.

Don't separate yourself from the oneness of your spirit with God; stay connected. Walk in unconditional love for your brothers and sisters and with nature. God speaks to us in so many ways. I don't believe anyone alive can reside in the spirit realm all day everyday but I do know one thing for sure – the more I'm connected to God the more difficult it is for my flesh to wander around all loose and reckless.

"Those who live according to the sinful nature have their minds set on what nature desires; but those who live in accordance with the Spirit have their minds set on what the Spirit desires. The mind of a sinful man is death, but the mind controlled by the Spirit is life and peace; "
Romans 8:5-6

12

The Joy Of Waiting

Patience means the willingness to stay where we are and live the situation out to the full in the belief that something hidden there will manifest itself to us.
Henri J.M. Nouwen

Patient people move the world because they understand that everything is a process. We are all on a journey of enlightenment, even before we realize we are. The journey requires that we experience certain things to yield a specific result/lesson. You can't hurry up the process. My older son's due date was in July but he wasn't born until August; there was nothing I could do but patiently wait until he arrived.

It looks like the world is moving so fast but it is all an illusion; a trap to get you to move faster and faster and faster. If you're moving faster and faster and faster you have no time to think about what you are doing and what is actually happening to you. Slow down!

In many states a right turn at a red light is permissible after a full and complete stop. After receiving a ticket in the mail accusing me of running a red light by one of those hidden cameras I no longer assume I can make a right on red; so now I'll sometimes sit through a red light – just so I don't get any more tickets. Well, when I do the people behind me become irate. They honk at me, wave

83

their hand out of the window in anger and one person after realizing I wasn't going to turn on red literally drove around me at the light. They risked their life, my life and the life of any pedestrian walking across the street just to not have to wait. Impatience can kill you, literally. What is so important that you can't wait a moment?

Sometimes your patience can be tested by those who are closest to you. The more you exercise patience, the more people will think you are a pushover; when in actuality you are stronger than they are. Patience takes an enormous amount of internal strength.

There is no such thing as time in the spirit realm; remember, we are all spirits who possess a soul (mind-will-emotions) and live in a body. Conflict arises when our spirit self and our carnal self desire polar opposite outcomes. Our spirit self is willing to take all of the time it needs to learn a lesson, but our carnal self wants everything right now, right now, right now! Those in control of this world understand our carnal weaknesses and gladly feed us the pleasures of our flesh – impatience.

"My dear brothers and sisters, take note of this: Everyone should be quick to listen, slow to speak and slow to become angry." *James 1:19*

Do not be conformed or seduced by wanting everything right now – let life and any challenging situation play itself out. Everything that happens in our life happens for our greatest good and that promise from God ensures us that our endurance is not a weakness but a valued treasure to be honored. True wealth belongs to those who are patient.

How To Feel More Positive

You have brains in your head. You have feet in your shoes.
You can steer yourself any direction you choose.
You're on your own. And you know what you know.
And YOU are the one who'll decide where to go...
Dr. Seuss, *Oh, the Places You'll Go!*

Norman Vincent Peale transitioned in 1993, according to his website, he pioneered the merger of theology and psychology which became known as Christian Psychology. He dedicated his life to the message of positive thinking. Your thoughts are vibrational energy that transmits to the universe on varying levels. Positive thoughts take place at a higher vibrational level while darker thoughts are much more grounded. People who are consistently positive are thought to be very nice people, angels even. They are regarded differently in our society – they are given more because they exude patience and positivity. The good news is that everyone has that ability; the key is whether we choose to reside in a higher vibrational level or a lower vibrational level. God is no respecter of persons (our carnal selves); living positively lightens your load. Negative thinking makes the load heavier to bear on your journey.

Do an attitude adjustment. It doesn't have to happen overnight, we all know that everything takes time.

Negative thoughts are poisonous and sneaky. Negativity takes hold in your body little thought by little thought and moves you out of the spirit realm one unchallenged negative idea at a time. If you find yourself thinking negatively cancel that thought. Just say it, "I cancel that thought!" You can cancel anything; yes, even your thoughts.

The more positive your thoughts are the more work God can do to release you from anything that binds you. It is very important that you turn all your negative feelings into positive ones. When you feel the opportunity to shine, never hold back. Let your light shine!

Your blessings are waiting for you just outside of your comfort zone.

Staying positive while you're being stretched is never easy. But know your reward is right there waiting for you, just on the other side of mass discomfort. Stay positive and claim whats rightfully yours. Let go of the act and stay true to yourself. This will help you to stay on track with your own personal goals. Think for yourself to find passion and motivation. Once you have passion and are motivated, you can do anything. Enjoy the discovery of how great your life is.

Fear keeps us in our comfort zone – it's time to grow. Isn't it comforting to know that we can be positive through any situation because it's all going to work out for our greatest good in the end? God's grace will carry you during your low vibrational moments – don't get stuck there, your life depends on it.

Freedom From Fear, Negative Thoughts and Negative People

Dance with your fear.
Anthony Robbins

Are you a host to God or a hostage to fear? Fear is a sense that alerts you to discomfort or the unknown. It's not about overcoming fear but welcoming the discomfort and the unknown into your life. No one wants to be uncomfortable – that's why the mattress industry is big business. Once we accept our life is a journey of ups and downs and lessons to be learned discomfort and the unknown become something we deal with, like morning breath.

God has gifted animals and humans alike the innate ability to have a heads-up about something coming our way that is out of the ordinary. When the hairs rise on your neck and your ears sharpen and your shoulders begin to heighten and roll back you do in fact need to be aware; not retreat, but be aware. Fear doesn't necessarily mean danger – it just means something is coming your way that you probably have not experienced in this way before.

When I was pregnant with my first son I was terrified of giving birth. The thought of having a whole body come out of the tiny hole that was used to get him in there really terrified me. I remember asking my midwife if I could be asleep for the delivery. She assured me that everything would be okay and since I was young and healthy my body would respond well to the vaginal delivery. She eased my fears and baby and I made it through just fine. When the time came for me to deliver my second son I wasn't afraid at all. I was more afraid of being responsible for two little people (because I had never done that before) than actually pushing him out. Again, fear alerts us to discomfort and the unknown, my fears with baby number two were very different because I was about to journey to a place I had never been before – being the mommy of two little people.

Discomfort and the unknown can cause an increase in heart rate and blood pressure, tightened muscles, dilated pupils, decreased ability to focus and worst of all mental and physical paralysis. The spirit of fear alerts you to a discomfort or the unknown; it is not an enemy to fight. You can never overcome fear; it's about acknowledging the source of your discomfort, embracing the unknown and dealing with those issues. Fear is a sense, not an actual thing that can be fought or battled.

Finding out *why* you feel afraid is the beginning of your free life. Remember, fear is not something to battle; fear is a gift that nobody wants. Fear is a helper to keep you aware and on point. It lets you know that something is coming your way – not necessarily good or bad, but something that will make you grow or something you've never experienced before. Fear is the opposite of faith – believe in your heart that everything happens for your greatest good and you'll never be afraid again. Fear is a spirit, like love, and is designed to help you successfully navigate your journey.

No one wants to live their life in constant worry or anxiety, a free flowing life is one that provides exponential opportunities for growth and liberation. Here are a few tips to help you better grasp the gift of fear:

👍 Remain positive.

The most effective means to overcoming your fears is to change your perspective and behavior towards it. Since that may not be easy to do, you need to keep yourself motivated. Fears that produce a negative reaction to your mind and your body have roots in your negative thoughts and outlook in life. Brush aside those negative ideas from your mind and always remember that everything that happens to you is for your greatest good.

👍 Communicate with your Spirit.

There is no better person who knows more about your fears than your spirit (your internal self). Engage in dialog with your spirit to more quickly and easily identify fear when it comes upon you. Break down your major concerns into digestible portions so when fear does come you're better equipped to maneuver that pivotal moment.

👍 Ask yourself, "Are my fears based on anything I've experienced?"

Some fears are irrational and only take place in the mind. Most fears are caused by one's inability to have control over a given situation. If you ever feel this way, it's best to gather as much information as you can, the more facts you have in hand, the less you become stressed about your situation.

👍 Don't be afraid to fail.

Why are you afraid to fail? Do you think you may disappoint someone? Disappoint yourself, maybe? Well, guess what – failure is all about perspective of expectations. If everyone expects a student to earn a 100 on their exam and the student earns a 90, can we honestly say the student failed the exam? The failure only exists in the minds of those who expected a 100; but to the masses a 90 is completely acceptable.

Don't put unnecessary pressure on yourself. I believe that overall failure doesn't exist. I believe life is a series of tests and trials and pure judgment comes upon us when we transition to our next life; and even at that point failure doesn't exist. According to the bible in John 14:2, Jesus says, "In my Father's house are many rooms; if it were not so, I would have told you. I am going there to prepare a place for you." In John 14:3 he continues "And if I go and prepare a place for you, I will come back and take you to be with me that you also may be where I am."

The many rooms he is referring to are the different levels of judgment; so even in death there is no failure.

Unless you are able to let go of the fear of failure, you will never, ever achieve your full potential in life. If you think you can, you can; and if you think you can't you're right. Be brave and bold! Go for it all – shoot for the stars. God's got your back.

Consider professional help.

If you believe it is too much to confront your issues alone or without support then it is best to seek professional help. A professional coach, counselor, therapist or the like, will assess your abilities and suggest techniques that you can employ to move forward. Overcoming the root of fear can be a long process, so don't expect to get rid of all your fears (if you have many) at once. Understand that you have control over your life; whenever you feel afraid, tell the Universe, "Thanks for the heads up!"

"Your beliefs become your thoughts,
Your thoughts become your words,
Your words become your actions,
Your actions become your habits,
Your habits become your values,
Your values become your destiny."
Mahatma Gandhi
October 2, 1869 – January 30, 1948

Negative thoughts can rob you of life and steal years from your life. We will all experience highs and lows during our lifetime but the key is not getting stuck in those moments. When things are going poorly – remember you are just passing through; and when things are going well – remember you are just passing through. In all things give thanks and perpetually show gratitude for your life and everything you *do* have. It's easy to complain about what you used to have and what you think you should have but there are always people in the world with less than you.

When negative energy begins to rise within you immediately write down your feelings, no matter how long it takes you to get it all out. Then, fold the paper and place it in your 'negative jar'. Your negative jar can be an old coffee can or a beautifully decorated hollow book – you choose. You will find the process of extracting your negative thoughts (via writing) and ridding them of from your presence (literally externally) cathartic.

Meditation is another awesome way to rid your body-temple of negative thoughts; it brings together in perfect harmony your mind, your body and your spirit. When I first began meditating I just couldn't still my thoughts. I sat on a huge square pillow with my lower back up to and including my shoulders gently pressed against the wall, my legs were stretched out in front of me and my hands were placed palms down on the floor. The room was silent and I closed my eyes. My mind kept focusing on what I needed to get done as soon as I got up from the floor. I never attempted to calm my thoughts before and after a few minutes my tailbone began to hurt so I stood up and chalked mediation up to new-age malarkey. About a month later I tried to meditate again; and this time, after learning more about the process I was able to sit for a few more minutes. As I began to regularly meditate its soothing affects began to work, not just during my time of mediation, internal reflection and prayer but actually during my workday. Stilling my thoughts through mediation has afforded me the ability to better think things through, better manage my day and quickly tap into my inner strength when needed.

You may need to mediate a few times before you begin to notice small changes in your life. You will begin to feel more calm and peace-filled. You'll be given a fresh set of eyes to review old problems and best of all you will have connected with a higher energy and your higher self. As you develop your mediation skills you will discover how challenging it is to harbor negative thoughts about yourself and others. As you evolve into your higher self and shed negative thoughts, you'll begin to easily detect negativity in others. This doesn't necessarily mean they *are* negative people but your spirit will pick up on their negative energy.

Letting go is never easy, that's why there are so many shows on television dedicated to helping hoarders; but just as you're making a concerted effort to rid yourself of negative thoughts you may have to rid yourself of negative people as well. It's not easy letting go of negative people in your life; it's hard to kick them to the curb when all of their broken promises are accounted for. You may simply need to make a clean break, even when it comes to those who you love the most. If you are worried that you simply don't have it in you to let them go, then you'll need to get the support from others. Talk to your friends and ask them to help you find the strength to break free. It's easier to walk away from negative people when you have one or two people supporting your decision emotionally. If you seem to be losing more than you bargained for, keep in mind that friendships lost while trying to better yourself will rekindle if a true friendship really existed from the beginning.

Letting negative people go may feel like the worst thing you'll ever endure in life but eventually your life will improve and your soul (mind – will – emotions) will prosper. Not only will you be able to improve the way that you see yourself, but negative people, places and things will no longer hold you back from happiness.

Finally, consider what is best for you. Concentrate on your needs and wants rather than what others think you need or want.

$$\langle 15 \rangle$$

How To Feel More Confident

Obstacles are things a person sees
when he takes his eyes off his goal.
E. Joseph Cossman

Confidence is the heart of a con(fidence)-game; the victim becomes so taken by the grace and cache of the principal they don't even realize they're being taken for a ride. One of the key lessons to learn on our journey is being aware; in the spirit of *life being remixed,* take cues from where ever we can and use our newfound knowledge to move humanity forward.

It's all about your projection. When you learn how to accept yourself for who you are you'll be able to benefit even more from all of the experiences you have. There is a thin (and I mean thin) line between confidence and cockiness. The moment you go overboard and think everything is all about your world you end up looking like a jerk. There are many ways to express yourself and maintain the delicate balance between confidence and arrogance.

Dress your best even if you're just running out for 20 minutes.

I attended a business expo at the Jacob Javits Convention Center in New York City on a cloudy/rainy spring day; I knew I was going to be walking around for at least six hours so I wore a pair of skinny jeans, a black fitted t-shirt with a black lightweight knit blazer and my new black and lime green Nikes. I tucked my long hair under a cute hat and put on my shades and big silver hoop earrings for good measure. By all accounts I looked fine for someone walking around the city and a convention center. Most New York City events are far enough to take a cab but by the time you hail a cab and sit in traffic to get to your destination you could have gotten there faster by walking; and that's what most of us do. I felt I was perfectly suited for the occasion until I was given the opportunity to be interviewed on camera by a major cable channel business show.

"Damn!" I thought. Why didn't I wear a shirt with a collar and a necklace? There was nothing I could do about my wardrobe at that point so I just rolled with what I had on. I had no clue I'd be given this amazing broadcast opportunity and I took it. I was grateful to have makeup in my messenger bag, which I quickly applied, and thankfully it hadn't rained too heavily so my hair was manageable. Since my t-shirt was fitted and I did have on a blazer I was able to pull it off – they took a tight shot (filming of just my upper half) and I didn't look too badly on playback. I was able to make the best of the situation very quickly but that was a lesson for the record book. I don't care how much it's raining outside or where you have to walk – always leave your house looking the best you can. Although my outfit was okay, I know in my heart that a more professional look would have made me feel more confident.

👍 Speak well.

As a kid, my mom was relentless about my diction, grammar and vocabulary – it was a hassle to deal with growing up but to this day I am very grateful for her resolve. The ability to put a subject with a predicate and properly conjugate a verb positions me head and shoulders above many. I'm actually writing another book now on manners, decorum, etiquette and grammar. A good command of the English language will give you confidence to speak in front of a crowd or hold court with a small group. Speaking well with give you an edge over your competitors no matter what industry you're in.

👍 Get fit and exercise.

Maintaining a regular exercise regimen will change your life. Your mind will be more alert, your body will respond more quickly to impending dis-eases and your appearance will change for the better. I don't like exercising but I am in the gym getting my work-out on if not every day then every other day. If I'm traveling and I miss the gym for a few days I feel my body tightening up and I don't like that feeling. The better my body looks the more confident I am; the more confident I am the more money I make and the bigger a difference I can make in the lives of others.

👍 Carry yourself well and create your signature walk.

Would you ever want to conduct business or work with someone who has no oomph or get up and go? I sure don't. Always act like you have somewhere to go; have a sense of urgency about your aura and your affairs. Others will have more confidence in you if they believe you have places to go and people to meet. Put pep in your step and watch new opportunities come your way. Your walk and your body language all tell a story; what nonverbal story are you telling others about you. Good posture and a brisk walk tells others, "I am on it and if you want to connect with me you must be on it too."

Again, this is not about being arrogant, it's about making a few small changes in who you are to show the world you mean business and they must come to you correctly or not at all.

👍 Have humility.

Strong personalities have a tendency to command attention and respect everywhere they go; so in that vein it's very important to maintain a humble (not passive) spirit. Jesus rocked with the best of them and knew how to blend in where ever he went – to experience the most success on your journey it pays a King's ransom to be humble. When all of the other things are in place (diction, wardrobe, posture etc.) you may find yourself on an island because people are too intimidated to speak with you. The secret is exuding confidence while remaining humane and approachable.

👍 Be knowledgeable of current events.

When Sarah Palin was John McCain's running mate for Vice-President she was asked in an interview if she agreed with the *Bush Doctrine*. It was evident by her response that it was a "foreign" concept to her. The Bush Doctrine(s), at its core, is the fundamental belief in preventative war (let us get them before they even start thinking about getting us first, even though they may not want to get us at all) along with other foreign policy tenets as established by Bush himself and his administration. We all watched Sarah Palin's political career crash and burn during the campaign; perhaps, if she was a little more judicious in her studies of current events she may not have become the butt of countless jokes in front of a global audience. I believe she has absolutely no political future except to the die-hard Republican base, at best. For most people a multi-layered understanding of the *Bush Doctrine* and other foreign policies is neither necessary nor required to carry out their personal and professional responsibilities every day; but for someone who is charged with running our country, mastery level competence of our global relationships is of paramount importance. Be cognizant of important local, regional, national and international issues. They want you to be a sheep and not know what's going on. Fool them back and begin your own self-study plan; learn on your own, you don't need a college degree to read a daily newspaper. They want you to buy into a flawed system and become so dazed and confused that you don't have confidence in yourself or your thoughts. Tack back control of your life! The more control you have over your life the more confident you will become. It will exude from your pores and people will respect you more. The more respect you have the more confident you will feel. Don't let not knowing stop you. You don't have to get it right, you just have to get it going!

Be able to admit when you are wrong.

If you're able to admit when you're wrong, people will have more trust and confidence in you and your decision-making abilities should you ever find yourself on the wrong side of an issue. If you mess up at work, be the better person and (with confidence) admit to the fault; you'll earn major points with the Universe. Utilize all of your life experiences to move humanity forward one courageous step at a time.

Breaking Soul-Ties

Never make your home in a place. Make a home for yourself inside your own head. You'll find what you need to furnish it - memories, friends you can trust, love of learning, and other such things. That way it will go with you wherever you journey.
Tad Williams

The most important relationship you will ever have is the one with yourself; the second most important is the one you will have with others. How you interact with people, and under what terms really shapes your perspectives and who you eventually become. You are the average of your five closest friends. If they're always negative don't you think you will be also? If they tend to be happy and positive, don't you think you will be also? Be mindful of who you develop personal and professional relationships with. Once a bond has been developed, it becomes very difficult to break.

you -->

You are the average of your 5 closest friends.

Are you surrounded by people who really have your back?

Soul-ties develop when your mind, will and emotions connect with another person's mind, will and emotions; particularly on a deep and personal level. When you start sharing long conversations, your hopes, dreams, desires and wants with another person you are slowly developing a soul tie with them. A soul-tie is a spiritual connection between you and another person – male or female. You can experience unadulterated intimacy with someone without having sex or even touching their body. At this point, the soul-tie is developing; once you two become physical with each other an official soul-tie is established.

It has been documented that people can develop a soul-tie with an animal, which is bestiality. Soul-ties are very prominent between co-workers because they spend so much time together; remember soul-ties can be developed and even strengthened without a sexual relationship. For the record, those ties are easier to break – sex always complicates things. Gang members have soul-ties with each other and are bound by a loyalty that cannot be broken.

Sexual intercourse is mental and unites the engaged emotionally, spiritually, intimately through the mind and on even deeper levels through that act. When you deposit into other people and receive the deposits of others you begin to take on the essence of who they are into who you are; this is why people who are very sexually active are confused. Not confused, necessarily, about their sexuality, but because there are bits and pieces of so many others in their body-temple. You are forever changed after having sex with someone.

Professional sex workers are in business because their client has physically engaged with them mentally before the first touch or dollar has been exchanged. Men become intimate with women in their minds before they even approach her for intercourse and the same goes for women towards men. Be clear, soul-ties can be developed between same sex individuals just as easily as they're developed between males and females. I have a soul-tie with my best friend. She and I are always together and when we're not together we talk and text all day. We have never been intimate in any way but through our relationship I realize just how powerful soul-level connections truly are. When a soul-tie exists the physical act of sexual intercourse just seals the deal.

Some soul-ties are beneficial, like those between parent and child, mentor and mentee, leader and follower; those are examples of relationships where pure love and camaraderie is the glue that bonds them together. Love is the core of a healthy soul-tie; desire and loyalty are at the center and usually a driving force of an unhealthy soul-tie.

How to identify if you have a soul tie with someone

If you're wondering if you have a soul-tie with someone look at the fruit that relationship bares. Good soul-ties will bare good fruit; love, blessings, fidelity, honor, honesty and trust. The overall effect of a good soul-tie strengthens the essence of who you are. Are you in a relationship where violence, guilt, manipulation, hatred, resentment, fear, co-dependency, anger, or wrath abounds? Maybe, maybe not. Will others be hurt if they are made aware of your close relationship with this person? Perhaps. Do you do things for this person that you would never do for anyone else? Does this person take you out of your character? Does this person *ask* you to do things you normally would not do? Do their requests violate your ethics? If you can answer, "Yes" to any of these questions chances are you are in an unhealthy relationship and a soul-tie has been established.

How to break a soul tie

Breaking a soul-tie can and may break you. Breaking a soul-tie means addressing your issues on a spiritual level and that may take you to a place where you've never been before. Fear not! Prepare for tears and sadness but the joy of the Lord will be your strength. I believe the only way to get out of a bad situation where a soul-tie has been established is through prayer. It doesn't matter what faith you are or what religion you practice, this is one of those things in life that you have to pray your way out of.

Look to your Higher Power and repent (to turn around or apologize), look inward for strength to get out of this situation and be determined and focused to live for your greatest good – even if it means totally turning away from this person. You may or may not want to let the person with whom the tie has been established know that you are on your way out. You must make that decision based on your desire to get out. It's my prayer that you live a happy life free of cords and chains that tie you to nothingness leaving you and your destiny unfulfilled.

Self Care and Wellness

I think it pisses God off if you walk by the color purple in a field somewhere and don't notice it... People think pleasing God is all God care about. But any fool living in the world can see it always trying to please us back.
Alice Walker, *The Color Purple,* **1982**

Many of us fail to take care of ourselves – now is the moment we start putting as much care into ourselves as God does for the earth. Self-care doesn't necessarily mean getting your hair and nails done or buying new clothes at the mall; it means developing your inner self to be a light in the world – no matter what you may have on or what you look like. Looking good should be the result of you feeling good and not the other way around. So many people swear they have it altogether and their house is a mess, their lives are a mess and their kids are a mess; but as long as they look good nothing else matters. Here are some fun and affordable ways to care for yourself:

1. *Ask a friend to help you clean your house*
2. *Be grateful*
3. *Brighten up your wardrobe*
4. *Burn some tea lights or aromatherapy candles*
5. *Buy fresh flowers for your home or workplace*
6. *Clean out your email box and turn off your cell phone*
7. *Close your eyes and take a mental vacation*

8. *Color, draw, paint, scrapbook or create a vision board*
9. *Drink a lot of water and do a detoxification cleanse*
10. *Go for a long, leisurely walk*
11. *Enjoy a cup of herbal or loose leaf tea*
12. *Get rid of clutter in your house and in your mind*
13. *Give a hug (you'll also get one back)*
14. *Go out by yourself*
15. *Laugh and smile more*
16. *Meditate or take a yoga class*
17. *Touch yourself*
18. *Play music and dance*
19. *Reminisce through old photos*
20. *Replace a greasy meal with a healthy one*
21. *Send something to a friend in the mail*
22. *Sit next to a tree*
23. *Speak with an old friend*
24. *Write down your thoughts*
25. *Stop Smoking*
26. *Take a class to better yourself or start a new hobby*
27. *Take a bus ride to nowhere and back*
28. *Take a hot bath or long shower*
29. *Take a nap in the middle of the day*
30. *Start loving yourself because you're perfect just the way you are!*

The media has us razzle-dazzled thinking that only the rich can indulge. Not true, everything is relative; a $10 per month gym membership can be just as fulfilling as a $210 per hour trainer. You determine how you approach life, don't let someone or something else dictate how you feel about yourself and what you have (or don't have). God has everything planned out; all you have to do is walk in it.

18

Believe In What Matters

You change your life by changing your heart.
Max Lucado

One of my clients shared with me an argument she had with a business partner; "You don't care about what's important to me!" she shouted. "Because what you feel is important isn't important!" he shouted back. I thought his response was cold and very dismissive of her concerns but when you really think about it, how many of us make a big deal out of something that is not really a big deal. The mass media tells us what *they* believe should be important in our lives – constant updates on reality stars and American brides who go missing in the Caribbean – it's comical even.

It's important that you establish a belief system for yourself and determine what your non-negotiables are. Most belief systems are anchored in culture or religion; which is a great place to start, but by no means should it define your life "just because." In America, the primary religion is Christianity, and the laws of the land are based on such; a la the Ten Commandments. Of course, there is no law that states you have to be a Christian to live in America but in other parts of the world religion is the belief system and the law. Religion is never an easy topic to broach so perhaps this is the prefect area in your life to begin your private self-study.

Many of us believe in something, but if our faith doesn't line up with what we believe, for whatever reason, then we really don't believe in what we say we do. Our lack of faith in banks, government, churches, the media, our school systems and other long-standing institutions is ultimately leading to their demise. We believed in them and they betrayed us. Once someone has been betrayed and hurt at their core, the road to spiritual recovery is a long one.

When a loved one dies after hours of prayer it's probably difficult to even believe in God, right? I know, I felt that way when my mom lost her battle with ovarian cancer in her mid-fifties. It still hurts but I have stopped asking God, "Why?" I believe everything that happens to us is for our greatest good so why should I question the natural order of things because it didn't suit my fancy. I believe in God more now than before my mom died. I have to. I must!

Never allow anyone to tell you how to feel about God or religion, that's your personal choice and your cross to bear. Ask yourself, "Do I believe in God? Do I believe in the works of the Bible? Do I believe the Buddhist are right? Do I believe in the natural order of Mother Earth? What is it that I believe in right now?" It's important that you believe in something to have a compass for your life.

Travel the world or at the very least outside of your area code and see what else is out there. Don't shortchange yourself and believe what you are told to – explore the cosmos and believe in what feels best to you.

19

Restoring Hope

I knew, of course, that trees and plants had roots, stems, bark,
branches and foliage that reached up toward the light. But I was
coming to realize that the real magician was light itself.
Edward Steichen

Fear is a powerful emotion that will keep you living
in doubt and lack – bind that spirit and remain hopeful in
yourself and in others; move boldly and be the change you
want to see. President Obama's entire candidacy was built
on *hope* and *change*. He won the hearts of many across all
socio-economic lines. He was our modern day Jesus; the
one who came to restore. I have been extremely critical of
President Obama on some of his policy issues but one
thing I know for sure, is he has awakened a sleeping giant
– the soul of America and the world. During our crisis of
confidence his agility kept our spirits up; we have endured
a lot lately but President Obama made us feel like we had
a fighting change. Many dismissed his "hope and change"
message as endearing, in a most condescending way, but
that's what *we* needed to make it through another day. I
believe anarchy would have erupted if mass hopelessness
and despair was permitted to rest, rule and abide within us.

Remain hopeful and restored and not subjugated by
the evils in and of this world. Have we become so
downtrodden that we're grateful for any bone or scrap that

is tossed in our vicinity? Not even given to us, but tossed in our vicinity that we may fight our brothers and sisters for the paltry remains of their feast. There are forces in place that do not want you to be aware – they want you in a zombie-like trance so you don't even notice you are being led to the slaughterhouse. The slaughterhouse being the destruction of life, jobs, careers, belief systems, monetary systems and values as we know it. The seasons and the weather have been manipulated, earthquakes abound and volcanos are erupting with increase intensity – this is all deliberate!

Remain hopeful so that you may live an eternal life; remain hopeful for your own safety and sanity; remain hopeful so you can create a profound and lasting change in the lives of others. Remaining hopeful is not corny, wishy-washy or some esoteric mantra they teach in liberal colleges across the country; it is the guiding principle of the Universe in which we are all occupiers of.

Find peace and solace in the spirit realm, a space easily accessible through mediation and stillness. No one is crazy – people who are labeled crazy are enlightened spirits – they see more than the masses do; and in an attempt to stifle their voice are labeled crazy.

The best way to predict the future is to invent it.

Believe in serendipity, and in the strength of weak ties, connect with people from different fields and different places; use pattern recognition and peripheral vision to spot opportunities in unlikely places. In all things, remain hopeful that the best is yet to come.

◇20◇

Finding Your Passion

If you don't design your own life plan, chances are you'll fall into someone else's plan. And guess what they have planned for you? Not much.
Jim Rohn

Has anyone ever told you, "You are truly in your element," or "You are out of your element"? If so, feel grateful; God is speaking to you through them to offer direct guidance pertaining to the trajectory of your life. As you move about within your element, you'll notice that life seems effortless and without hindrance. Once you step out of your divine calling you become a projection of who others want you to be. Life is much simpler when you discover your passion, walk in your purpose and live each day to reach your destiny.

Finding your passion, personally and professionally, is the key to ensure lifelong happiness, contentment and good health. When you love what you do, how much money you have in the bank matters less. When you love what you do, you look forward to every moment and welcome each day with zest and excitement. When you love what you do, work and everything else in life will bring adventure, opportunities and satisfaction right to your doorstep.

To find your passion, you must give yourself permission to be free. Freedom in life does not equal irresponsibility; it's a precious and valuable gift you give yourself to loose the shackles of past pain, past experiences, hurt and regret. Be honest with yourself – learn your feelings. Do you really know what makes you happy and content? Take time to incorporate your thoughts and feelings, your sense of individuality, your weaknesses, strengths, the things that annoy you, excite you, what you do effortlessly and naturally into your daily thought process. Knowing what you want and having the courage to go for it helps bond your mind and feelings to really uncover what you were born to do and accomplish.

Many people leave their jobs and relationships because they feel unappreciated and drained – this is a clear indicator of poorly set boundaries. Proper boundaries were never set because you didn't know enough about yourself to set any. When I first started dating my husband he told me two things; #1) we are to never, ever argue in public and #2) if we were to have children and our relationship didn't last, I was to never, ever take him to court for child support. He was very clear from day one of his non-negotiables. My husband (for over twenty years now) was sure of himself coming into our relationship; I, on the other hand, was very inexperienced, definitely not sure of who I was and was unable to set my boundaries because I didn't know enough about myself when we started dating. We married four years after we began dating and as I came into my own I started telling him what my rules were. At that point it was almost too late. We were already four years in and both of us were accustomed to the Saideh of four years ago, not the Saideh who was now a bride and a mom. Thankfully we made it past the hurdles. We were passionate about making our relationship last so a little fine-tuning along the way and some give-and-take from both of us has kept our marriage going. I love the security and contentment that marriage brings but it would have never lasted this long if we were not passionate about making it work and willing to modify our beliefs along the way.

Passion expresses love in its purest form, serving as a conduit expressing goodwill to others while blessing the giver at the same time. How does your passion about your career or personal cause contribute to the greater good? If your passion is not blessing humanity or yourself, ask yourself why? Could it be that you are afraid? Love rests in the center of your passion. Are you afraid to love yourself? Could it be that you are afraid to love others? Don't let real or perceived mistreatment from parents, teachers, former employers, co-workers and other people keep you from owning your passion and expressing love in the purest form. These fears oftentimes can restrict our minds from being free, expressing love and living a passionate life. Don't live your life in fear – you are robbing yourself and cutting your life short by days and weeks. Have hope!

When you liberate yourself from negative thoughts and unpleasant past experiences, you will become more open to experiences that will transform you into a more mature individual; someone who is willing to accept the responsibility of changing their life through their own free will.

To find your passion think about what matters to you the most.

What are the things that really matter to you the most? What is your definition of success? Most working adults confess to experiencing a disconnection between their job and doing what they are really passionate about. Many of these same people experience irregular sleeping habits and stress. Work is not just an eight-hour interruption of the day, it is 1/3 of your day and over 50% of your waking hours. Find your passion and incorporate it in your job, if you can. Whether you like it or not, you are affected by choices you make at your job. How you act at work is often the most documented record of who you are, what you stand for, and what you believe. Success, for most people, boils down to abiding in a sacred space governed by passion and love.

When you were young, you thought anything was possible, right? Now it probably seems like you're stuck and have nowhere else to go. Clear your mind of all the negativity that clouds your emotions, take bigger risks and claim more than what you think you deserve. You have a life of possibilities ahead of you, if that's what you want. The lives we lead are based upon the decisions we make – are you leaning towards dread and doom or hope and vitality? Sometimes, I know, it's difficult to look at the glass half full when things just don't seem to be working out in our favor. Stay on the path! Remain hopeful, I have been there, trust me things always work out in the end.

I remember when I decided to get my body in shape. Whew! I didn't know what I was in for. Becoming healthier, losing weight and retraining my eating habits was the most difficult thing I have ever done in my life. I joined the gym and I was ready (at least I thought I was). It took me six years to gain thirty pounds and I got pissed because I couldn't lose it in three months. You see, I started with the wrong expectations; I thought I could take a few pills, work out once a week and eat a little less food and the pounds would melt away. Lie! I became depressed because I believed I failed and I quit going to the gym. After about six months and a few more pounds I decided to take another shot at getting my body in shape. *This time* I had the passion to win!

Getting fit almost became an obsession. I started out by going to the gym as frequently as I could, so instead of coming home and watching television I'd head to the gym and take a class or just walk on the treadmill. It was a start. One day I decided to take every class the gym offered for a week, that way I could see what classes I liked. Oh my, after a few days I was in so much pain I thought Jesus was going to come down and escort me to heaven. I cried every day that week but I went back the very next day. I knew this portion of my life's journey was not going to be easy but I had the passion to win. I was not able to take every class the gym offered that week because I was in so much pain so it took me about two weeks. Once I found the classes and the instructors I liked I was hooked. Desire got me *to* the gym but my passion for a better body has kept me going.

See, everybody wants to avoid pain, we are designed that way. Comfort is what we all seek even if it's to our own detriment.

After three months of consistently taking classes and walking > jogging > running on the treadmill I noticed that my clothes no longer fit. "This is odd," I thought. The scale says 176.6 but all of my clothes are swimming on me. I started out at 182 pounds so I was happy with my six pound weight loss but I knew something else was going on with my body.

After consulting a fitness professional I was told that one pound of muscle weighs the same as one pound of fat but muscle takes up less space in our bodies; my muscles were tightening and taking up less space in my body so I was actually looking smaller even though I weighed the same. This was amazing news to me. My passion took over where I lacked knowledge. Fitness is not my area of personal or professional strength, but I knew one thing, there was no way I could exercise and my body not kindly respond. I didn't know what my body was going to do, how it was going to look or what the results were going to be, but I knew the Universe had to respond because my mind, my desire and my passion made an unspoken agreement that this needed to take place in my life. In three months I went from a size 14/16 to an 8/10! I purchased a pair of jeans and put this picture on my Facebook wall to encourage someone who may need inspiration in this area. God always uses me to inspire and encourage others.

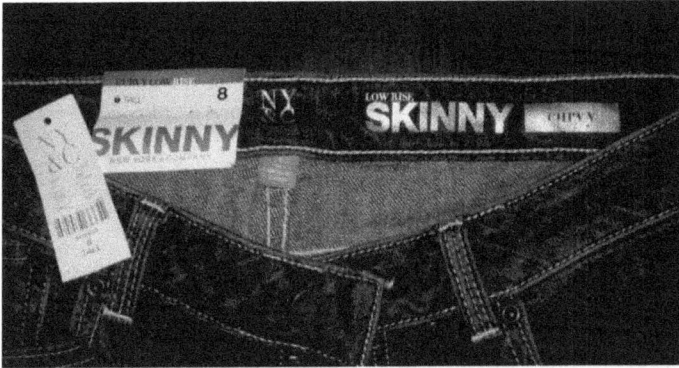

Follow your heart and dreams and strive to find your passion. When you do this, you'll experience a transformational leap and a deeper connection with the Universe. Each person has a unique journey and the discovery of their passion plays a major role in who you ultimately turn out to be. World-renowned essayist Ralph Waldo Emerson has sum up the things that define an individual's success, I pray you find inspiration through his words:

Success

To laugh often and much; to win the respect of intelligent people and the affection of children; to earn the appreciation of honest critics and endure the betrayal of false friends; to appreciate beauty; to find the best in others; to leave the world a bit better, whether by a healthy child, a garden patch or a redeemed social condition; to know even one life has breathed easier because you have lived. This is to have succeeded.

📄 To find your passion, identify your strengths and values

Knowing yourself and feeling confident begins with an accurate understanding of your strengths and values and what makes you feel good about yourself. The process starts by evaluating the factors that molded the person you are today such as your family, past experiences, education, and trainings. I knew I wanted to be an entrepreneur since I was seven years old even though I didn't know what an entrepreneur was. I'd tape and staple books and other doo-dads together and sell them to my grandmother and grandfather. They'd give me a nickel and of course pretend that buying from me was their greatest joy in life. So I'd go back and make some more stuff and sure enough, they'd buy that creation as well. Money was never the motivator – I was stimulated (at seven years old) by the experience of making something and selling it – the joy of their purchase fueled my passion (at seven years old). By the age of seven I was following my passion and my grandparents encouraged me. Never step on a child's dream, ever. Perhaps at seven years old you didn't have what I had, but if you really reflect back on your life I'm sure there were people along the route helping you get to where you needed to be. As we get older, we become more cynical and are not as accepting and gracious to the gifts and words others bring to us. Imagine yourself back at seven years old with my grandparents encouraging you; what would you be doing now? Now...put your doubts on a shelf and go for it!

Knowing your top top-five strengths and non-negotiable core values gives you a template by which you measure choices in your career and personal life. Being successful in life means you can freely use all of these strengths as well as fulfill your values. Understand that forging ahead into new and unchartered terrain is not easy – life is not easy nor was it designed to be easy. Be encouraged. Just as my grandparents encouraged me, I am here to encourage you.

You are stronger than you think you are! God strengthens me. God can strengthen you too. Please know there is a force much bigger than we could ever imagine working things out on our behalf, we just have to go through the process. When a woman delivers a baby vaginally she is literally squeezing a body through a canal that is centimeters wide; giving birth causes a tremendous amount of pain. But after the pain and after the process is complete a beautiful baby is born. God is always working things out on our behalf but we must be strong enough to endure the pain through the process.

You are smarter than you think you are! I used to tell my children, "I was born at night, not last night" when they were trying to get over on me. My older son was born during the summer between my senior year of high school and my freshman year of college during a time in my life when I thought I knew everything. Looking back...I realize I knew nothing, not even how to boil an egg. No, seriously, I was a little pampered and sheltered as a child and didn't even know how to boil an egg. But one thing was for sure, I had to grow up very quickly and soon realized that life didn't care what private school I attended, where I vacationed with my parents or what my SAT scores were.

Life wanted to know how I was going to feed my son, where we were going to live and how I planned on successfully making it through my first semester of college. I had to use my smarts and grow up fast. My ability to think and quickly process the facts helped me maneuver those first few years on my own. I actually turned out to be smarter than I thought I was.

A few years later my second son was born, I was now married and had to move things into high gear. I returned to work a few months after he was born but that just didn't fit well with my spirit. I saved up six months of paychecks and quit my job; yes, the same job that was paying a very nice salary and provided benefits and bonuses. My spirit told me it was the right thing to do, contrary to every human rationale as to why I should stay. To this day it's difficult to explain the feeling I had in my stomach in between the time I decided to quit and when I actually did. I questioned myself many days and sleepless nights, but I just knew it was something I had to do.

We are all much more intuitive than we think we are. To make ends meet I started any and every side business that came my way, all the while, my children were right there with me. If I had to attend a meeting outside of normal school hours my children attended as well. My entrepreneurial prowess developed and I got better and better at making money. One of my endeavors, a beeper store, afforded my family luxuries, trips and a lifestyle I never imagined for myself. Had I not quit my job my life would have taken a totally different path. Quitting my job was one of the many decisions I've made in my life that was totally driven by intuition. We are all much more intuitive than we think we are. Rely on your intuition – it is your internal compass. Oftentimes we are dismissive of intuitive thoughts because intuitive thoughts counter all aspects of logic, reason and rationale. So what! The more developed and educated we become as a society the less we feel the need to rely on God's direction (intuition).

During the early part of June 2008 I was at home on my computer and I heard the word *radio* flow into my left ear. I literally looked to my left to see if someone was standing next to me – no one was there. "Huh," I thought. Where did that come from? I Googled the word *radio,* not even knowing what I was looking for and one of the top links in my search result was a press release that a new Internet radio station had just received a four million dollar round of funding. I clicked on the link, read the article and followed another link to the actual company's site. It was a new Internet company that allowed ordinary citizens to host their own online radio show for free.

On June 26, 2008 I launched Life Remixed Radio, a one hour daily radio show that featured *today's hottest topics from a faith-based perspective.* I called in every favor from every entertainment contact I had to make the show work. Within the first month I interviewed Play from Kid N Play, many authors and movie stars. My biggest "get" was when I interviewed Teena Marie; she sang and prayed on my show. The day she transitioned the radio station featured my show in her honor. My show became very popular and my cache skyrocketed, all because I didn't ignore the whisper into my left ear. Since the launch, I have renamed the show *The Sai Browne Morning Show,* never thinking I would have a career in the media. My intuition has never let me down. The only downside of always following my gut is falling out of favor with people. Because I am led and guided by my intuition some of the decisions I make don't make people happy; like canceling things at the last minute or simply not getting involved with projects that, according to logic, seem perfect for me. Then there are those projects that I do get heavily involved in that have little or nothing to do with my brand or what I'm working on, but God told me to get down with it – so I do. I have learned that my intuition is never wrong. The more I rely on my intuition, the stronger it has become. I challenge you to begin listening to that still small voice that whispers directives into your spirit – follow it and see where it takes you. God's got your back! Never forget that.

There have been times when I listened to God, followed the directions and found myself in what I thought was the worse place ever. When my mom died of stage IIIc ovarian cancer I launched an awareness campaign in her honor. Through my connections, I was able to produce a cancer awareness event at Madison Square Garden in New York City (yes, the same place the New York Knicks basketball team plays). Since this was for my mom I wanted to make it a huge event so we could raise a lot of money – I titled the event *Gospel at the Garden* and partnered with the WNBA's New York Liberty women's basketball team. I called everyone I knew in the gospel industry and started working to make the event happen.

Now, understand this...the whole event was born from my desire to raise awareness about the dreaded cancer that took my mom's life; however each move was directed by God. I heard, "move left" and I moved left; I heard, "call this person'" and that's just what I did. Before I knew it I was speaking with heads of entertainment companies, radio stations, Madison Square Garden executives and normal everyday people. I cursed God daily the two months leading up to the event! I didn't know if people were coming at me because they liked me and what I was doing, I didn't know if people were coming at me because they wanted my contacts, I didn't know if people were coming at me because they thought I had a lot of money....it was awful. I privately threated to cancel the event damn near every day until it happened. I never fully understood the magnitude of the event until it was actually over, then I realized how much power I had inside of me that was laying dormant waiting for an opportunity like this to be released. You are much more powerful than you think! God lives within you and strengthens you every day. You are powerful beyond measure – don't look for an opportunity to become powerful, listen to those whispers and create your own opportunity. Power comes from our legs, our arms, our minds and most importantly, our hearts. God has the power to show you who's God, never lose your heart or love for people, their plight and their needs. You will be given enough power to start and finish what task God needs you to do. Trust and believe and you will be more powerful and influential than you ever could have imagined for yourself.

After the dust settled from *Gospel at the Garden* I was left to clean up the fragments of broken relationships, disjointed friendships and pine through pages of financial reconciliations, I thought I'd never see the light of day. I stayed on task doing what I knew needed to get done. It wasn't easy but I was more resilient than I originally thought.

You are more resilient than you think! We all have the ability to bounce back. Listen, if you are taking direction from God you most assuredly will be given the power to make it through. As you travel on your journey there will be many opportunities for personal growth and expansion; you will experience many hurts and disappointments but you have everything you need inside of you to bounce back. God's got your back, trust the process and trust the execution of the plays. You will never, ever be led astray.

What are some of your greatest strengths?

_____

_____

_____

_____

_____

_____

_____

_____

_____

_____

_____

_____

_____

Now that you've spent time discovering your greatest strengths, how do you plan on using them to become more successful personally and professionally?

_____

_____

_____

_____

_____

_____

_____

_____

_____

Now that your strengths and how you plan to better use them for success have been identified it's time to identify your non-negotiable core values. Your non-negotiables help you stay committed to what you believe in and are typically aligned with your purpose in life. These tenets, if repeatedly compromised, will most assuredly take you out of your character, down the wrong road and get you distracted from your purpose.

One of my non-negotiables in life is to never be in a friend's wedding. I have three close friends whose nuptials caused a fraction in our relationship; one of which caused a complete breakdown and demise of a longstanding friendship. I don't do weddings, period. The key is learning about yourself and knowing enough about yourself to make your journey has harmonious as possible. It's not about running from tough decisions or avoiding pain, but about using your free will to create the life that you want and not live a projection of what other people want for and from us.

What are your non-negotiable core values?

_____

_____

_____

_____

_____

_____

_____

_____

_____

_____

_____

_____

Learning who you are is painful and during the process you may shed some tears but as you learn more about yourself you'll open up to possibilities and opportunities that were not evident to you before. Some people hide their true strengths out of fear of rejection; no one can reject you but you. Now that you have assessed your strengths and values, you can better find your passion.

Tips to help you uncover your passion

Some people take a lifetime to realize what they finally want to do with their life; it took me exactly ten years. The revelation was rendered to me on April 29, 2002; the release of this book, on April 29, 2012, culminates my ten year journey in the wilderness. The day this book is released is the day I begin walking in my true destiny and am no longer a vapor but the manifestation of God's predestined plan for my life. It's not easy figuring out what to do for (and with) the rest of your life; I, like many others, pursued my passion only after I endured several failures. How many alternatives must we test before we get it right?

"Americans can always be counted on to do the right thing...after they have exhausted all other possibilities."
Winston S. Churchill
November 30, 1874 – January 25, 1965

There are so many things to think about and issues to be settled before it finally becomes clear about your passion and what you really want to achieve. To help you in this regard, here are some tips that you can follow:

Set Goals

You must perform a self-assessment and outline a goal setting process to map out where you want to go in life and how you plan on getting there. Really put some thought into what you have gone through to reach this point in your life? Where are you right now? And what else do you want to happen? How do you perceive yourself two to three years from now? If that goal is not possible within the next few years adjust the dates further out to maybe five or ten years; then go deeper and come up with other short term goals. Don't wait; start working on your plan now. I recommend creating a worksheet for every single goal you have. Grab a sheet of paper and create a chart that looks like this (the numbers in the parenthesis are there for reference only, you do not need to number your goal sheet):

(1) Objective		
(2) Start Date	(3) End Date	(4) Why these dates are important
(5) Change Partner	(6) Partner's contact information	
(7) What I need to do / Phase One		
(8) What I need to do / Phase Two		
(9) What I need to do / Phase Three		
(10) How I plan on accomplishing this goal		
(11) How I know my plan was successful		

(1) Clearly define your goal – before you can start moving and shaking things up, you must know what you want. If you have more than one goal you'd like to accomplish use a separate sheet. You may even want to print several goal sheets, punch holes in them and keep them in a handy binder.

(2) Indicate the day you plan on starting the journey of completing this goal. Remember, in life you must always finish what you start.

(3) Indicate the date you plan on accomplishing this goal. The key here is to be realistic. If it took you 3 years to pack on an extra 15 pounds, please do not expect to lose those extra pounds in a week.

(4) Knowing *why* you are doing something is just as important, if not more so, than actually getting it done. Your *why* is what keeps you motivated.

(5) Having a change / accountability partner is critical in accomplishing your goal. This person loves you and really wants to see you succeed. Keep their email address and phone number handy at all times. You don't want to look for phone numbers in the middle of a breakdown. Keep in mind that you are not an isolated being; rely on those necessary to help you reach your goals.

(6) (7) and (8) I recommend that you break down your goal into three phases; now, some challenges are going to be much more complex and may require more thought out planning. This chart is designed to get you started, feel free to modify it to your specific life as you see fit.

(9) This is the step that holds most people back; knowing *how* they plan on accomplishing their goal. Remember we talked about heavily relying on intuition, well, this is the line item that is dedicated to that expression of love from God. The key is to outline your process for accomplishing your goal which creates an unspoken agreement with the Universe. Now the Universe has a starting point to begin feeding you the answers. You must start somewhere and once you do, the Universe will supply every resource and provision for you to accomplish your goal.

(10) It's import you establish from the onset how you will be able to determine if you were successful or not. Movement without purpose is like a hamster running on a

131

wheel – you'll get very tired very quickly only to realize you're in the same place you started.

Below is my goal sheet for writing and publishing this book – I trust it will add further insight to help you get your plan started.

Objective	*Write the book Life Remixed*	
Start Date *December 2011*	End Date *April 2012*	Why these dates are important *I need to have the book done by my 10 year anniversary*
Change Partner	*my husband, I can call his cell anytime, and doesn't really like email*	
What I need to do Phase One	*Pull together all of my notes and scraps of paper and type them into the computer, even if it's just a few words on a single page*	
What I need to do Phase Two	*Write every day – organize content everyday – even if it's just for 15 mins.*	
What I need to do Phase Three	*Find a graphic designer, editor and printing company*	

How I plan on accomplishing this goal	I plan on writing as much as I can and adjusting my workload to ensure the book is retail ready by my desired publishing date
How I know my plan was successful	I will know I was successful when I sell a copy of the book on April 29th!

While on the journey don't forget to give yourself time for pleasure. Don't neglect life because you are too busy chasing your goal. Life is about balance. To find your passion you must allow yourself a time for pleasure.

For many people, allowing pleasure into their lives induces feelings of guilt that pleasure is a nonproductive hindrance from getting important things accomplished. This view of pleasure is subjective. Pleasurable moments are good for your health and are necessary to maintain productivity. By allowing yourself time for pleasure you become more focused and passionate about your life and where you're headed.

Expand Your Horizon.

Take a look around you. What do you see? Do you see the same-old, same-old thing or do you see what's really possible for your life. Take a trip, if you can, and see how other people live. If you're unable to take a trip drive to a town 25 miles away – if you're unable to do that, take the local bus to the last stop. Do whatever you need to do, but at the very least, get out of your usual surroundings whenever possible. I live in New Jersey and commute into New York City like thousands of people do; it's nice to drive in but sometimes I find more pleasure taking public transportation. I enjoy watching people, hearing what teens are talking about, and really remaining aware of hot topics and trends via local conversation.

What creates a spark in your heart? What inspires you to move forward? Go after more of that. What is pleasing to your eye? Use objects and people to help you figure out what really matters to you and go for it! Open up your senses; when you open up your senses, you will experience more of God's blessings and feel more peaceful and serene. This allows you to be more patient and be reminded of the cycle of nature. When you experience these moments you'll become more positive and calm and your spirit will become more receptive to new thoughts and ideas.

You have to take risks in order to know your capabilities. Don't be afraid to fail, that's part of the game. Learn from your own mistakes and grow from them.

👍 Take money out of the equation.

God knows what you have and what you need. Don't let what appears to be a lack of money hold you back from getting ahead. Money is not the cure-all. When we don't have the amount of money we'd like to have we tend to believe that money will get us to where we need to be; that's not necessarily true. God is not in the counterfeiting business; the bible says in Proverbs 13:22, the wealth of the wicked is stored up (or passes to, in some versions) for the righteous. Money has to circulate – it has to find its way to you, and trust me it will. Money is an enhancer and allows you to do more of what you already do - good, bad or indifferent.

There have been many projects I've worked on over the course of my career and more often than not, I didn't have enough money to complete what I needed to do. But in almost every instance, money found its way to me so I was able to get done what I needed to do. Don't be discouraged, or feel dismayed by what appears to be lack of one of the many resources in your arsenal. If you don't have enough money, use the resources of your contacts. If you don't have the right contacts begin networking more. If you don't have the money to go out and network, use social media and that's free. If you don't have immediate access to a computer, visit your local library. If that's too much for you to do then you may not be ready to meet your destiny yet.

Today is the day to stop thinking about what you don't have and be more grateful about what you do have. There is no lack or limitation in your life, freely you give and freely you receive from the storehouse of God. Don't let your heart be troubled by the appearance of lack. God is there for you and ready to give you everything you need, expand your mind and be open and receptive to having what you need to succeed whether its cash money or resources.

👍 Make a dollar and a difference.

Being gifted with money and resources is a blessing. When they both come your way, which they will, what are your plans? Do you intend on serving yourself or serving others? Remember, money has to circulate; it's not yours to hold onto. Use all of your resources to enjoy your blessing and to be a blessing to others.

Finding your passion is an endless song. When you do the things that you are passionate about you allow life to flourish in and around you. Let yourself connect to everything you are – in mind, in heart, and in spirit. Become stronger so you can better face challenges that come your way on the journey. Stay alert and alive and determined. Your passion can take you places you never thought you could go. Your passion is the guiding light of your spiritual journey; finding your passion does not promise an easy life, rather a rich life open to hope and possibilities.

What You're Breakthrough Looks Like

Success is falling nine times and getting up ten.
Jon Bon Jovi

When you experience a breakthrough, you literally shift into another dimension. The dimension is not higher or lower per se, but a different space of consciousness.

Your breakthrough occurs the moment you realize that following your intuition has led to a series of recognizable victories! **It's an awareness that spiritual systems and laws work and are far superior than human systems and laws.** Its when you know, beyond a shadow of doubt, that the spirit realm is more real than the space we occupy with other humans on a daily basis.

Your breakthrough is a spirital orgasm that you never want to end. You may get the chills and cry and maybe even rock back and forth. It's that intense. You will become overtaken by a love so strong that you feel it in the pit of your stomach. You'll experience euphoria – the embodiment of heaven on earth. You will become so filled with love for God and love of self that you may find yourself speaking in a language foreign to you, and that's okay too. Let love flow and reign in your life. Everybody's breakthrough moment happens differently and in different ways; and is certainly not confined to a church or typical place of spirituality.

Before and after your breakthrough, you may experience intense moments of clarity (also known as "ah-ha moments"); those are love seconds with God designed to redirect your soul (mind – will – emotions) back to your predetermined path which is your destiny.

Often times our breakthrough happens right before we are just about to give up. Don't give up. God is with you on your journey. Trust your Higher Power and follow your intuition to delight in the results of your obedience.

22

Walk In Your Purpose At Any Age

What you think is working against you,
is actually working for you.
Bishop T.D. Jakes

Many believe that globalization, technology and tough economic conditions have moved us collectively away from our purpose in life; I believe *because* of those factors we're able to step back and truly see what our purpose is. No one is too old or too young to go where they really want to go. If you surrender to defeat, you'll die never knowing what you could have accomplished in life.

As a child our dreams, fears and belief system are established by our parents (or lack of parents), our community and cultural norms. As young adults our lives become a continuance of the mandates that were placed on us growing up. One day, all of us will ask ourselves,

"How did I get here?"

"What am I doing here?"

"Is this really what I want to do for the rest of my life?"

"Is this where I want to be?"

"What is my purpose in life?"

These are solid questions that many of us didn't start asking ourselves until we realized we took the wrong road two or three times. The good news is its never to late and you're not too old to walk in your purpose.

👍 You are not your job.

We have humanized our job beyond the task it really is. Breathe life into a career – the thing you'd do for free because it makes you feel so good. Just because you have a great job and it fulfills certain financial needs in your life doesn't mean you are walking in your purpose. Do not relegate your whole self to what you do for a living.

Most of us were told go to school, get a job, enjoy an annual vacation and don't ask questions; and that's what we did. We hunkered down and did what we had to do. Duirng that proces, however, we became more and more identified by what we do to earn a living as opposed to using our available resources to become more of what we were meant to be. You are not what you do for a living. Your job should provide resources to amplify your purpose, not replace it.

👍 Pay attention to your own life.

When you arise each morning, be grateful to God that you have another chance to get it right. A lot of people didn't wake up this very morning. Pay attention to your life – what is your body telling you? What color are your eyes? What shade is your teeth? When did you start drinking coffee and why? Does milk give you gas? Does pizza sauce give you heartburn? Do you enjoy sex in the morning or the evening? What is the optimum water temperature for your bath or shower? You love your children but do you like them? What is your life telling you? It's telling you something but we have busied ourselves into a drunken stupor. Stay fully present in each moment. Taste every ingredient when you're cooking – you'll enjoy the final meal even more. Feel every lick and stroke during lovemaking – you'll enjoy your orgasm even more. Take deep breaths and feel God's ever presence – your life will become more peaceful. Life has so much to offer, don't let is pass you by without so much as an acknowledgement from you.

Learn from life experiences.

Tony Robbins said, "Life happens not *to* me but *for* me." Learn from every single chapter in your life. You are not a victim; you are a strong person who has learned from your experiences. Something in life has given you a glimpse of your possibilities. Go back to that vision and reflect about what in that moment made you smile.. That's your passion! Your passion becomes your destiny.

Experience life

Discovering your purpose in life is not an intellectual experiment that can be dissected and stored for later research and use, is involves trial and error, knowledge of self and your belief that you are here for a reason. Life begins at the end of our comfort zone. You may be fearful but don't let it overtake you and stop you from experiencing new and exciting things. Be bold and do something you have never done before. Your past doesn't matter! Take a cooking class. Walk a mile. Fix your own plumbing. Fill up your car with gas and drive until it's empty. Who says you can't...ususally it's just yourself.

👍 Follow your heart.

Age doesn't matter when it comes to pursuing what will make you feel complete; just ask 70 year old newlyweds. Follow your heart no matter what it looks like to others. Following your heart means following the God in you and you should never ever have to justify your Godself to anyone. Yes, you may have priorities that prevent you from taking a huge plunge now; that only means you need to be more methodical in your approach. Go ahead and think if you must. Your brain wont explode. We're talking about some pretty radical maneuvers here – take your time if you must.

Some people never get the chance to look back; they died before they had a chance to live. Don't be that one who dies before they have a chance to life. Walk in your purpose so when you take your last breath you can go in peace because God will whisper in your ear, "Well done my good and faithful servant."

Section

Three

⚜

Be Unstoppable!

Accept Your Assignement

Focusing your life solely on making a buck shows a certain poverty of ambition. It asks too little of yourself. Because it's only when you hitch your wagon to something larger than yourself that you realize your true potential.
Barack Obama

It took me the better part of ten years to finally come to terms with the truth that God can and *wants* to use me for something greater than I ever saw for myself. Someone once asked me, "How much do you need?" I thought about it for a second and responded, "About ten grand."

"That's it?" he said. "Yeah, I'm not picky, I really don't need anything but if I did ten grand would cover it." That was before I received my first check for ten grand!

God wants so much for us but we place limits on ourselves that needn't be there; all while subconsciously granting our mind, with the help of our emotions, permission to keep us in our comfort zone just steps shy of our destiny and success.

There is an awesome story in the bible of Samuel and how he learns God's voice and accepts his call:

1 Samuel 3:1-10 *The Good News Translation*

[1] In those days, when the boy Samuel was serving the Lord under the direction of Eli, there were very few

145

messages from the Lord, and visions from him were quite rare.[2] One night Eli, who was now almost blind, was sleeping in his own room;[3] Samuel was sleeping in the sanctuary, where the sacred Covenant Box was. Before dawn, while the lamp was still burning,[4] the Lord called Samuel. He answered,

"Yes, sir!"[5] and ran to Eli and said, "You called me, and here I am."

But Eli answered, "I didn't call you; go back to bed." So Samuel went back to bed.

[6-7]The Lord called Samuel again. The boy did not know that it was the Lord, because the Lord had never spoken to him before.

So he got up, went to Eli, and said, "You called me, and here I am."

But Eli answered, "My son, I didn't call you; go back to bed."

[8] The Lord called Samuel a third time; he got up, went to Eli, and said, "You called me, and here I am."

Then Eli realized that it was the Lord who was calling the boy,[9] so he said to him, "Go back to bed; and if he calls you again, say, 'speak, Lord, your servant is listening.'"

So Samuel went back to bed. [10] The Lord came and stood there, and called as he had before, "Samuel! Samuel!" Samuel answered, "Speak; your servant is listening."

The Lord went on to deliver a vitally important message meant specifically for Samuel. The next morning Eli pressured him to tell what the Lord spoke the night before – it was a damning message for Eli and his family.

Upon hearing the news Eli said, "He is Lord; let him do what is good in His eyes."

At the time Samuel was serving under Eli so, in theory, Eli could have received the message sans Samuel since the message was about him anyway. But, as we learn from the rest of the story, Samuel was the only person who could receive that message and was then charged with governing himself accordingly armed with the knowledge given directly to him from the Lord. Samuel accepted his assignment and the pressures that came with it.

There are so many take-a-ways from this bible story; let's start with the obvious. God was trying to connect with Samuel but since Samuel had never heard from Him on his own he didn't even know what the voice of the Lord sounded like. The story tells us how Samuel, a boy at the time, labored for the Lord under the direction of Eli, so when he was lying in bed and heard his name being called he rightfully assumed that it was Eli calling him. It wasn't until Samuel came to him three times that Eli realized the voice Samuel was hearing was that of the Lord.

Learn how God speaks to you.

It took a few years, but I finally learned how God communicates with me. God tries to connect with us in many different ways, it's up to us to keep our lives as clutter free as possible so we can a) quickly identify when a message is coming in and b) process the message and properly apply it as directed. The Lord continued to communicate with Samuel as he grew up and he was later attested as a Prophet. Even if your assignment has nothing to do with religion or spirituality relish those love seconds with God to redirect your soul (mind – will – emotions) back to your predetermined path which is your destiny.

> Follow the instructions given to you even if you don't understand them.

Just follow God's directions – your life will be so much easier in the long run. Besides, God is giving us directions to benefit the greater good and our self-directed life is governed by our limited purview. To understand the journey of success is to understand and accept that it is not about us.

The 4ᵗʰ Watch; 3am-6am

Heaven is under our feet as well as over our heads.
Henry David Thoreau

I was born into an Islamic family, yet attended church faithfully as a child. I follow the teachings of Dr. Creflo A. Dollar and the easy-to-understand lessons of Joyce Meyer. I swear by the Sunday morning preached word at "bedside-baptist" under the leadership of Bishop T.D. Jakes and I'm always encouraged by Pastor Joel Osteen. I like Cardinal-Archbishop of New York Timothy Michael Dolan because he has a sense of humor. This past Palm Sunday I attended Jehovah Jireh Praise and Worship Christian Center in Newark, New Jersey with my friend Celeste; I drove to my grandmother's house immediately after service to give her a few palms while shouting "Hosanna" and listening to the live version Pastor Marvin Sapp's classic song *Never Could Have Made It.* I follow a lot of what Oprah says and I do believe that Ekert Tolle is onto something. So, where does that spiritually leave me?

I was raised to believe that God is up in heaven somewhere keeping score of our life; and all we can do is hope that when we die the good-deed list is longer than the sins-I've-committed-list and we can make it into heaven. That's what many of us have been led to believe.

After a chance meeting in 2001 with Hip-Hop icon KRS-One, at the signing of the Hip-Hop Declaration of Peace at the United Nations, be began working together. We worked well together and after a short time moved both of our families to Atlanta to open the global headquarters of the Temple of Hiphop (he spells *Hip-Hop* as one word to symbolize unity within the culture). In an instant I became the executive director of an organization with over 25,000 members worldwide.

On April 29, 2002 I was enjoying a birthday lunch from one of my friends in one of the most celebrated venues in Atlanta and was told that God needs me. "Huh, really, now," I thought. "Did you have too much to drink already?" It was the middle of the afternoon and we had a whole day to go. "You're nuts," I said.

"No, Sai. I'm serious."

The conversation sobered our mood. I detailed the entire experience in my first book *From Hip-Hop to Heaven* but in the spirit of *Life Remixed* I can say that my life changed forever at that moment. Many people seek God and search their whole lives for something that was seemingly placed in my lap. The laundry list of things I could no longer do was extensive. "Why me?" was all I kept asking. The only answer I ever got back was, "Because." I was, however, given a choice. I was told I could follow the directions I would be given and allow God to use me or continue my life as I was; but if I chose the latter, I'd die a thousand deaths. Sigh. That wasn't much of a choice.

During the months that followed, I received extensive insight and revelation about my life, my history and the future. KRS and his family moved to California and I stayed in Atlanta with my family trying to navigate my new normal. I spent most days hoping to die and one day I tried to.

I moved back to New York a year and a half later still trying to understand why God chose me. During the move I found one of my bibles and written on the inside back cover dated August 1999 was a note I wrote, in essence, asking God to come into my life. Immediately it hit me! God didn't just intrude on my life – I asked for it! I asked for something big and I got it! Every moment and situation, post August 1999, was directing me to April 29, 2002. I didn't realize it because my spiritual teaching as a child positioned God as an entity that we had to beg, not a spirit that will lovingly and willingly give us everything we ask for. I wasted so much time being angry, bitter and resentful instead of just accepting this new role in my life. There was so much for me to understand and (re) learn and I had no one to turn to but God – I wasn't asking easy-to-answer questions.

Upon moving back to New York, I took a year off to do nothing but think and I had a lot to think about. I was beginning to accept my role as a spiritual leader but still wasn't quite sure what that looked like. I was told by my guide the things I should not do, it was up to me to figure out what I needed to do to advance the mission based on the mandate that had been given to me. My life was saved from destruction so I could save others.

God gave me direction, but not directions.

As my spiritual studies deepened I noticed how I began to know things before they happened. During a conversation with another mom about child safety I recalled an incident from my childhood where a 6 year old boy had been kidnapped a block and a half from his home. At the time of the kidnapping I had just turned 8 years old and lived just a few blocks from where the kidnapping took place over 30 years ago. Two days after our conversation, a breaking story hit the news, New York City police and the FBI began excavating an apartment building a block away from the little boy's home based on new evidence about his disappearance. For a second I was shocked and then my entire body smiled. God had given me a gift.

The more I looked to God for directions, the more I was directed to the spirit realm. This is not about ghosts and things that go bump in the night – but about better understanding that spirits dwell among us every day and reside in another dimension. We are all spirits mastering a human experience – we are not flesh and body first – we are spirits who possess a soul (mind, body and emotions) and live in a body.

This is deep and why I believe churches focus on religious practices and social issues such as homosexuality, birth control and pre-marital sex. Those are important and relative topics, but there is so much more for us to learn. I believe, in large measure, churches and institutions like the government and colleges and universities exist to keep the story going on varying levels. I know I'm not the only person who wonders why we never fully address the real issues affecting our world; it's because they don't want us to, period. Both of my children are "askers" and question everything; both were labeled "disruptive" throughout their school years. Why? Because they wanted to know more than what was being fed to them. It becomes a real problem when you question the status quo and then question some more. If churches really delved into the spirit of God they would be labeled foolish or find that they too have been duped in many ways.

I feel spirits, I see things when I am wide awake, I've been told that orbs can be seen circling around my head, I've been told that I glow. So many times when I'm out shopping random people walk up to me for assistance, I wish one day I could shout back, "Do I look like I work here!" I exist to help others. I am a light in dark places because I unwittingly asked for it, my heart and intentions were pure when I made the request. Much is based on our intentions and our thoughts. God knew I could handle the job. As my connection with God has deepened over the past ten years I've come to appreciate the many ways God connects with me. God connects with us many of the following ways:

💧 Nature

👓 Things we see

👂 Things we hear

🗨 Conversations with others

📖 The Bible

☎ Receiving a 3am wake-up call

The manner with which God connects to you may not work with me and vice versa. There are many ways God connects with us and most are universally and easily understood, but the one that baffled me the most was consistently waking up around three in the morning.

The bible shares few stories about the significance of 3am but makes many references to morning and daybreak; which we can glean in this day and age to be between the hours of 3am and 6am. The following story in the book of Exodus chapter 19 explains God on so many levels; how communication happens, how instructions are rendered, how instructions should be followed and more specifically why God embraces the obedient.

¹ On the first day of the third month after the Israelites left Egypt —on that very day—they came to the Desert of Sinai. ² After they set out from Rephidim, they entered the Desert of Sinai, and Israel camped there in the desert in front of the mountain.

³ Then Moses went up to God, and the LORD called to him from the mountain and said, "This is what you are to say to the descendants of Jacob and what you are to tell the people of Israel: ⁴ 'You yourselves have seen what I did to Egypt, and how I carried you on eagles' wings and brought you to myself. ⁵ Now if you obey me fully and keep my covenant, then out of all nations you will be my treasured possession. Although the whole earth is mine, ⁶ you will be for me a kingdom of priests and a holy nation.' These are the words you are to speak to the Israelites."

⁷ So Moses went back and summoned the elders of the people and set before them all the words the LORD had commanded him to speak. ⁸ The people all responded together,

"We will do everything the LORD has said." So Moses brought their answer back to the LORD.

⁹ The LORD said to Moses, "I am going to come to you in a dense cloud, so that the people will hear me speaking with you and will always put their trust in you." Then Moses told the LORD what the people had said.

¹⁰ And the LORD said to Moses, "Go to the people and consecrate them today and tomorrow. Have them wash their clothes ¹¹ and be ready by the third day, because on that day the LORD will come down on Mount Sinai in the sight of all the people. ¹² Put limits for the people around the mountain and tell them, 'Be careful that you do not approach the mountain or touch the foot of it. Whoever touches the mountain is to be put to death. ¹³ They are to be stoned or shot with arrows; not a hand is to be laid on them. No person or animal shall be permitted to live.' Only when the ram's horn sounds a long blast may they approach the mountain."

¹⁴ After Moses had gone down the mountain to the people, he consecrated them, and they washed their clothes. ¹⁵ Then he said to the people, "Prepare yourselves for the third day. Abstain from sexual relations."

¹⁶ On the morning of the third day there was thunder and lightning, with a thick cloud over the mountain, and a very loud trumpet blast. Everyone in the camp trembled. ¹⁷ Then Moses led the people out of the camp to meet with God, and they stood at the foot of the mountain. ¹⁸ Mount Sinai was covered with smoke, because the LORD descended on it in fire. The smoke billowed up from it like smoke from a furnace, and the whole mountain trembled violently. ¹⁹ As the sound of the trumpet grew louder and louder, Moses spoke and the voice of God answered him.

²⁰ The LORD descended to the top of Mount Sinai and called Moses to the top of the mountain. So Moses went up ²¹ and the LORD said to him, "Go down and warn the people so they do not force their way through to see the LORD and many of them perish. ²² *Even the priests, who approach the LORD, must consecrate themselves, or the LORD will break out against them."*

²³ *Moses said to the LORD, "The people cannot come up Mount Sinai, because you yourself warned us, 'Put limits around the mountain and set it apart as holy.'"*

²⁴ *The LORD replied, "Go down and bring Aaron up with you. But the priests and the people must not force their way through to come up to the LORD, or he will break out against them."*

²⁵ *So Moses went down to the people and told them.*

It was then that God spoke the Ten Commandments to Moses.

Verse 16 says; *On the morning of the third day there was thunder and lightning, with a thick cloud over the mountain, and a very loud trumpet blast. Everyone in the camp trembled.*

This is significant because God told Moses in verse 11 this is how the Lord would be revealed to the people.

Upon further reading in the bible you will find Jesus praying around this same time of day. Mark 1:35 says, "Very early in the morning, while it was still dark, Jesus got up, left the house and went off to a solitary place, where he prayed." This was his period of restoration.

In the next verse we read where Simon and his other companions went looking for Jesus, when they found him Jesus said he was ready to head to the next town to preach because that is what he has come to do. Jesus, fully aware of his assignment, spent countless hours and days fulfilling the mandate placed upon his life but he too needed a place of solace and renewal.

I believe, based on scripture, research and my own 3am moments that 4th watch is the most sacred time of the day; I believe the veil between our world and the spirit realm is the thinnest during this time and is our purest opportunity to connect with God as closely as we can while on our human journey.

I am awakened many times between 2:57am and 3:04am and 3:27am and 3:33am by my doorbell ringing, a knock on my bedroom door, garbage cans being dropped between my house and my neighbor's house, a noise in the kitchen, and various other noises that if heard at any other time of day would make someone check it out to see what's going on. When I kept being awakened by these noises around the same time each night I knew something spiritual was going on.

One's 3am awakening cannot in anyway be attributed to race or class or gender – it is a gift from God designed to encourage you to walk in your faith, submit to prayer and be open and receptive to the messages you'll receive. It's important to know that you may not get an answer during your time in prayer; the answer will most likely be dropped in your spirit over the next few days. One thing I can guarantee is God is trying to reach you. Be like Samuel and just say, "Speak Lord for your servant is listening."

You're not crazy and your awakenings have nothing to do with your body's internal clock, gas, last night's dinner or sleep apnea. It is God, pure and simple, trying to connect with you because you reached out asking for help at some point via your thoughts or actual words. Embrace the moment. Find a quiet place like Jesus did and accept whatever insight you are given. We are living in very difficult times – be thankful that you have a spiritual advantage. Every advantage helps.

> Journal your thoughts the next time you are awakened around 3am to better understand what God is telling you.

_____

_____

_____

_____

_____

_____

_____

_____

_____

_____

Be Unstoppable!

The shoe that fits one person pinches another;
there is no recipe for living that suits all cases.
Carl Jung

I saw an interview a few years ago featuring Will Smith on Tavis Smiley's talk show and during the interview Mr. Smith says, in response to a series of questions about his success, "I am not afraid to die on a treadmill." Mr. Smiley, in a gentle attempt to add clarity to that statement, suggests that what Mr. Smith is really saying is that he will not be outworked. Mr. Smith says emphatically, "I will not be outworked, period. You might have more talent than me, you might be smarter than me, you might be sexier than me, you might be all of those things; you got it on me in nine categories, but if we get on a treadmill together, right, theres two things. You're youre getting off first or I'm gonna die. Its really that simple." Now, as a person who finds no pleasure of any moment spent on a treadmill, I tucked that precept into my memory bank.

Not long ago I came to the conclusion that I needed help managing my weight and food intake, like many of us have done I joined a gym. Having that gym tag on my key ring validated the *mental* commitment I made with myself to eat healthier and take better care of my body. But, having a gym tag on my key ring simply wasn't enough to *physically* get me to the gym. Each month I was reminded of the broken commitment to myself when the recurring fee was deducted from my account. Finally, I had had enough and was serious about getting my health in order, weight and food intake included. I posted on Facebook, "the pickins' get slim after 40 so ladies get your butt in the gym!" Sometimes we'll post anything on Facebook.

A few days later, the spirit world opened up for a millisecond and showed me a vision. I was standing in my kitchen washing dishes and in an instant time stood still and I got a glimpse of my future. I saw myself outlined in yellow/gold, fully clothed and in motion. At first I was looking at myself straight on, I was only about three or four inches high and as I was looking at myself, myself was looking back at me; my little self smiled at me, turned to my right, its left and kind of skipped away smiling. That was one of the most surreal things I've ever experienced and it all happened in what was probably less than ½ second. I saw myself fit and smiling and a peace came over my spirit and my physical body. It *felt* right. I knew there were things I needed to accomplish in my life and being fit was going to play a major part.

The next day I went to the gym, picked up a group fitness schedule, chose the classes I wanted to take based on their descriptions and rearranged my entire schedule for the following week to accommodate the classes.

After the first few days I kept saying to myself, "What the hell am I thinking. I'm fat and it's going to take forever to get myself together." I wanted to talk myself out of going to the gym but I was literally afraid to. The vision

I had in my kitchen was too real to ignore. I never even bothered to try to explain and understand that moment with any of my friends. My desire to manifest the spirit and energy of that vision far outweighed my desire to continue my poor eating habits and slow, steady and consistent weight gain.

After taking a few classes with a few different instructors I settled in on my favorites – its odd, you know, how each instructor is given the same set of movements and music yet delivers them so differently. Rocky's Body Combat class is my favorite next to Alton's Zumba class. Rocky has this style that is so uniquely his own, there is something spiritual about the way he leads our class. Like he's been through some stuff in his life and is sharing his victory with us. And he does this in each and every class. He cares, he motivates and inspires. One day, as I was on the floor excruciatingly weak from working on my core he shouted, "Be unstoppable!" I collapsed on my mat and started to cry. I looked around hoping no one noticed. Since everyone was on the floor and dripping with sweat I think I just blended in. It's not like he's never said motivating things to us before but the inflection in his voice coupled with my spiritual agreement to pull my life together usurped the last bit of old energy from me. I cried because I knew I was on the right path, I cried because I remember Will Smith saying the other person was going to get off first or he was going to die. I was finally ready to accept the mental and physical encounter with death so I could live again. That moment on the floor changed my life forever. I was spiritually and physically unstoppable.

Most religions mandate a declaration – the moment you decide to publicly adopt the tenets of that belief system and dedicate your life to its higer power. My cousin's took their Shahada, as Mulsim's do but I got "saved". Getting saved is, according to Romans 10:9 in the bible, "...confess with your mouth, 'Jesus is Lord,' and believe in your heart that God raised him from the dead, you will be saved..."

I made the public declaration believing that I was now able to live in heaven for eternity; the moment was full of smiles but my heart felt the exact same as it did before my moment of salvation. The bible tells of many laying in prostrate (*adjective 1. Laying down, often on one's face, either out of respect and submissiveness; 2. lying down in a horizontal position due to illness or lack of energy; 3. Physically exhausted or emotionally overwhelmed; verb 1. To lie down or throw oneself on the ground especially in a worshipful manner; 2. To exhaust, either physically or emotionally*); and I truly believe laying on the floor in Rocky's class was that moment for me.

Become a life-long learner.

We all have room for growth, development and improvement, that's what life is all about. Life-long learning happens naturally unless the body and mind becomes unwilling. As long as a person is breathing, he or she must never cease from learning. Don't let your college degree lull you into a false sense of security; complacency is your enemy – fight it to the bitter end. Anyone who believes that credentials are enough is sadly mistaken. Each day technology changes how we do everything; don't fight technological advances embrace them. Confidence is everything in our global society; lack of knowledge will ding your confidence and set you back. There is no time for that. Be on point, use your accumulated wisdom to see what's next; accumulate more wisdom so you can survive and make it through this fast-paced world. Put it in your plan to read and write daily. Those who have continued learning throughout life, either in or outside of a formal classroom, will most certainly take in more of what life has to offer because they are open and receptive to everything that God has for them.

Live! Do not worry.

Worry is something we all do. Worry robs us of natural energy, and makes our life a living hell. For this reason, the bible offers us in Matthew 6:25-27 "Therefore I tell you, do not worry about your life, what you will eat or drink; or about your body, what you will wear. Is not life more important than food, and the body more important than clothes? Look at the birds in the air; they do not sow or reap or store away in barns, and yet our heavenly Father feeds them. Are you not much more valuable than they? Who of you by worrying can add a single hour to his life?" Further, Philippians 4:5-9 offers "Let your gentleness be evident to all. The Lord is near. Do not be anxious about anything, but in everything, by prayer and petition, with thanksgiving, present your requests to God. And the peace of God, which transcends all understanding, will guard your hearts and your minds in Christ Jesus. Finally, brothers, whatever is true, whatever is noble, whatever is right, whatever is pure, whatever is lovely, whatever is admirable

- if anything is excellent or praiseworthy - think about such things. Whatever you have learned or received or heard from me, or seen in me - put it into practice. And the God of peace will be with you."

👍 Think like an ant.

Have you ever tried stopping an ant but without killing it? You will see that ants have some qualities that people can learn from. If we embraced the perseverance, determination and focus of ants every once in a while, we would truly be unstoppable! Ants don't accept impediments or roadblocks, and you cannot stop them from trying to get around, go under or over whatever obstacles they encounter and are in its way. If you put an ant in a sealed jar, you will notice that it will try to find its way out by moving anywhere until it lies dead. A person who is focused has the mindset of an achiever. A person who is determined will not put off his or her responsibilities. A person who perseveres will always win even if they lose.

👍 Be disciplined.

Self-discipline is your ability to get on track and stay there. Laziness and procrastination are evil spirits and must be fought. You have what it takes! Tap into your inner power to defeat those spirits. Start with a solid plan to achieve your goals - including a time table. Then get organized; buy whatever you need to buy and rid yourself of everything you need to rid yourself from and get it done. Stop with the excuses and make it happen.

As I travel, I meet so many people who share with me their dream of writing a book, some have been working on their manuscript for over ten years; so I ask them, "Why isn't it finished?" And I usually hear five minutes of excuses. The number one reason why people don't get their book written and published is because they don't sit long enough to get their thoughts and ideas out of their head and onto paper. Once it's on paper, professionals can come in and take over – but the one thing professionals can't do is get the book out of their head.

If God tells you to do something, and you don't do it you are being disobedient and opening yourself up to the ills of the world. Be disciplined to complete every task you start, stay with it until it's finished. That's where your reward is stored.

👍 Allow time to heal all wounds.

Life is full of disappointments and hurts and the worst thing you can do to yourself is to simmer in your pain. You have to let it go! Let go of past hurts and misery or you will slow down your travels. I remember when my mom lost her battle with ovarian cancer – I counted each passing day after her death. I'd tell people, "My mom died 73 days ago," or "It's been 92 days since my mom died from cancer." I dealt with my loss the way I dealt with it but I stayed in that space far too long... she was gone and I was spending my life counting the days since she's been gone instead of trying to bring more life to the people who are still here. I stopped counted around day one hundred and twenty something but it still grieves me from time to time that my mom is not here anymore. Dealing with a loss is never easy. That's why it's so important to develop personalized coping mechanisms so when you do feel some kind of way you can quickly rebound.

Love is the greatest force there is and losing a lover or a special relationship can presumably feel worse than death by a thousand paper cuts. You miss the person, you wonder what they are doing, you may get angry, you may cry and feel sad – don't not acknowledge your feelings but don't live in a space of misery either. Acknowledge how you're feeling and move on. Your life depends on it. It gets easier with each passing day. The more time that passes, the easier it is to continue on your journey and enjoy new blessings coming your way.

I miss my mom immensely, and probably no less now than the day after she transitioned, but time has proven to me that I have to live on. I can miss her with all of my heart while staying fully present in the here and now so I don't miss any moments with the people who are still with me.

Time is a gift that God gives us; all we have is right now and none of us knows how many *right-now* moments we have left. Spend your time wisely – focus on how you can do more for yourself and for others. Time is the band-aid that comforts the pain of your loss or other wound. Let it do its job.

If you've lost your job or have experienced some other professional set-back, take the moments that you have and use them to develop your mind and your body.

Don't waste precious moments on bitterness and anger towards past bosses and co-workers. Do you really think they are thinking about you? I doubt it. They have moved on and you need to as well. It sounds simple, but I know it's not easy. Life is not easy. The journey is not for the faint at heart. Anyone can exist in life – it's easy to be a sheep and led by another – its more difficult to take control of your thoughts and your emotions and channel that energy for the long road ahead.

With every passing moment God gives you more insight into what you need to do and should be doing with your life – don't battle with God. Let the past go and move on. I love my mom and some of my past friendships and relationships that are no more but I know God has so much more for me and the longer I linger in yesterday the more I miss right now.

Success is a journey, not a destination.

During our lifetime we will experience challenges because there are lessons to be learned. Enjoy your never-ending journey of learning, healing and mastery of your calling. Never stop loving; never stop giving; never stop forgiving to live a long, blessed and prosperous life.

Thanks God, and so it is.

Amazing Grace

Amazing Grace, how sweet the sound,
That saved a wretch like me....
I once was lost but now am found,
Was blind, but now, I see.

T'was Grace that taught...
my heart to fear.
And Grace, my fears relieved.
How precious did that Grace appear...
the hour I first believed.

Through many dangers, toils and snares...
we have already come.
T'was Grace that brought us safe thus far...
and Grace will lead us home.

The Lord has promised good to me...
His word my hope secures.
He will my shield and portion be...
as long as life endures.

When we've been here ten thousand years...
bright shining as the sun.
We've no less days to sing God's praise...
then when we've first begun.

Amazing Grace, how sweet the sound,
That saved a wretch like me....
I once was lost but now am found,
Was blind, but now, I see.

John Newton (1725–1807)
Published in 1779

Saideh Browne has changed my life because...

_____

_____

_____

_____

_____

_____

_____

_____

The Prayer of Protection

The Light of God Surrounds Me.

The Love of God Enfolds Me.

The Power of God Protects Me.

The Presence of God Watches Over Me.

Wherever I Am, God Is,

Wherever You Are, God Is.

AMEN